HISTORIC PUBS
OF LONDON

She was nuts on public-houses, was England's Virgin Queen. There's scarcely a pub of any attractions within ten miles of London that she does not seem to have looked in at, or stopped at, or slept at, some time or other. I wonder now, supposing Harris, say, turned over a new leaf, and became a great and good man, and got to be Prime Minister, and died, if they would put up signs over the public-houses that he had patronized: 'Harris had a glass of bitter in this house'; 'Harris had two of Scotch cold here in the summer of '88'; 'Harris was chucked from here in December 1886'.

No, there would be too many of them! It would be the houses that he had never entered that would become famous. 'Only house in South London that Harris never had a drink in!' The people would flock to it to see what could have been the matter with it.

Jerome K Jerome, *Three Men in a Boat*, 1889

HISTORIC PUBS
OF LONDON

TED BRUNING

PHOTOGRAPHY BY ERIC WELLER

PASSPORT BOOKS
NTC/Contemporary Publishing Group

This edition published in 2000 by Passport Books
A division of NTC/Contemporary Publishing Group, Inc.,
4255 West Touhy Avenue, Lincolnwood (Chicago), Illinois
60712-1975 U.S.A.

Jacket design by Bob Eames
Design and photography copyright © Prion Books 1998
Text copyright © Ted Bruning 1998
Text design by Jill Plank
Photography by Eric Weller, Design on Camera

Printed in Singapore
International Standard Book Number 0-658-00502-2
Library of Congress Catalog Number: on file
01 02 03 04 15 14 13 12 11 10 9 8 7 6 5 4 3 2 1

CONTENTS

HISTORIC PUBS 6

HISTORIC
PUBS

MAKE a list of things you think about when you think about London, and along with Beefeaters, Buckingham Palace, red buses and black cabs, pubs are bound to be near the top. So much of London's history is caught up in them: so many names of the city's past, Marlowe, Pepys, Dr Johnson, Dickens, Thackeray, Chesterton and Orwell are intimately linked with its pubs.

The architecture of the public house has uniquely preserved the physical fabric of the domestic life of generations past: the George in Borough High Street, London's only surviving galleried coaching inn, fantastically antique as it may seem to us, was as prosaic as King's Cross Station to the travellers of 1676; while the gin-palaces of the latter half of the last century were the everyday resorts of everyday people.

It's this continuity of use that makes London's pubs so central to an appreciation of the city and its history. Amid the Square Mile's glass

Above Samuel Pepys – frequenter of pubs and London's most famous chronicler

canyons, the high-rise blocks of the East End, and the warehouses of Wharfland, you will find pubs which date back 300 years. Go into any City wine-bar and you will see businessmen talking shop, doing deals, or just taking a break as they have for centuries. Take a day-trip to Hampstead and nurse a pint of stout in the Flask, and you are relaxing just as 200 years of day-trippers have done.

The story of London's pubs really begins on 2 September 1666. Not that there had been no inns, taverns or alehouses before then; indeed, some thought there were too many, and there had been frequent, fruitless, attempts to curb their numbers. But scarcely one of them escaped immolation on that day – the day of the Great Fire.

The importance of the Fire derives not just from the destruction it caused, but from the act of rebuilding it unleashed – an awesome transforming energy. Before the Fire, London had grown little in extent in three centuries: there was the City, the seat of commerce; south-west, round a bend in the river, lay Whitehall and Westminster, the nation's political heart; south, across London Bridge, lay lawless Southwark with its brothels, its bear garden, its Wooden Os; east were the scattered villages still known today as Tower Hamlets. These districts were surrounded by blasted heaths where robbers lurked; by small towns, many with markets of their own; by the palaces and country seats of aristocrats and merchants; by the dairies, orchards, and market gardens which supplied London with its perishables.

The reconstruction that followed the Fire seems to have taught landowners that land was not valuable for the rents or the produce it yielded, but for its development potential. Soho, once a hunting-ground, was the first of the new areas to be built up, followed by Mayfair. Throughout the 18th century, London slowly spread outwards, more than doubling in extent within the lifespan of people who could remember the Fire. In the 19th century the process accelerated: from

Above Dr Johnson, a ubiquitous London imbiber, was patronised by a brewery owner

1811 to 1911 London's population quadrupled to 4,000,000 in an explosion almost as dramatic as the modern expansion of Mexico City, Djakarta or Cairo.

As London grew outwards, following the line of new railways and roads and then filling in the gaps, old towns such as Richmond and Brentford, once economic centres in their own right, were swallowed up; new districts such as Brixton sprang up on open farmland; and great houses and their parkland such as Balmes House in Hoxton vanished beneath the surge of brown-brick terraces.

But London's growth was not only a question of outward expansion. Internally, its character was constantly changing. Once-fine areas such as Spitalfields, originally settled by prosperous Huguenot weavers, decayed into crowded, vicious slums. Landmarks as well-known as Newgate Gaol were pulled down and built on. New roads and railways bulldozed through ancient residential areas. The City itself changed almost completely as office-blocks of imperial stature spread over the medieval street-plan and its classical buildings.

London's licensed premises are the great survivors in this process of expansion and renewal. There are examples – sometimes isolated examples, granted – from almost every period of London's history except the great medieval inns and taverns: Chaucer's Tabard and Falstaff's Boar's Head have long perished. But there are pubs scattered about the edges of the Metropolis which are clearly 16th century – the Crown & Treaty at Uxbridge is one. The 17th century has left us the Fallow Buck at Enfield, the Old Bull & Bush in Hampstead, the Hoop & Grapes in Aldgate. Coaching inns are few: the great inns of central London were all demolished in the 19th century, although there is always the George in Southwark. As for the taverns of educated 18th-century London, they are in many cases proudly preserved: are there many City pubs in which Johnson, Boswell and Goldsmith did not carouse? And in many cases even those genuine old taverns which did not survive were rebuilt in the sparse, manly style of the original, the Olde Cheshire Cheese in Fleet Street being a prime example.

Opposite Gin palace mirrors and lighting used to brilliant effect at the Camden Head

The secret of the survival of so many antique pubs is simple: as long as they were making money, there was no incentive to replace them. And as long as the likes of Dickens could make the drinking public believe in age as a virtue in its own right, the builders and operators of inns and taverns would strive to maintain an air of antiquity, authentic or contrived.

But just as London is, largely, a Victorian city, so London pubs as most perceive them are Victorian pubs; and the expression that will probably spring to mind is "gin-palace".

To understand gin-palaces, it is necessary to know that in the previous century there had been an explosion in the distilling and consumption of cheap, adulterated and often poisonous gin, comparable to the way crack cocaine has taken over the slums of North America. Hogarth's twin paintings, Gin Lane and Beer Street, express the view held by many legislators that gin was evil and beer virtuous.

So in 1830 the Government passed the Beer Act, allowing anyone to set up a beerhouse on payment of a token fee. The idea was to undercut the gin-sellers: almost overnight the price of beer halved as thousands of beerhouses were set up, many of them low dives in the desperate slums which were to be found all over London – a painful side-effect of its explosive growth.

Social conditions in Victorian London were unimaginable to the modern mind: in overflowing slums, appalling poverty, rampant disease, and unmanageable crime abounded. Overcrowding was perhaps the worst problem. Rooms were partitioned and sub-partitioned, let and sub-let. Small wonder that the 'dangerous classes' or 'surplus population' sought refuge in the bottle. All the symptoms of the gin epidemic were repeated, this time in the beerhouses: the slum-dwellers packed them to the doors.

By 1869 the Government had learnt its lesson, and repealed the Act. Most of the squalid drinking-dens disappeared; but those 39 years had been a gestation period for the pub as we know it, for in that time a number of variations had evolved in succession to the urban taverns of previous centuries – indeed, the very term 'public house' is a Victorian one.

Undoubtedly the most important of these variations was the gin-palace, but there were a number of others. Music-hall, for instance, was born in the concert-halls of the big beerhouses of the early part of the century, continuing a dramatic tradition in taverns dating back to the Middle Ages.

Catering was also important: businessmen and clerks, then as now, favoured pub lunches, and in business districts a good trade was done by dining-rooms and luncheon rooms – especially those which offered a sombre, old-fashioned atmosphere. Many still laid on a "shilling ordinary" into the middle of the century, but this communal meal with its atmosphere of Pickwickian good fellowship was giving way to the intimacy of separate tables. (Probably the last was at Simpson's in Cheapside, still running a one o'clock ordinary complete with chairman and a prize for guessing the weight of the cheese as late as 1926.) Fish restaurants were particularly popular in Victorian London, stretching along the Thames from Richmond to Greenwich; for the river, despite the pollution, still provided eels, whitebait, and oysters at four a penny. Foreign restaurants also came into vogue, eclipsing the native chop-houses: the Café Royal, Regent Street, in 1863, Kettner's in 1867 and Pagani's in 1871.

By and large, though, genteel folk regarded pubs with grave suspicion – often rightly. A prosperous publican in a seedy area – such as Stunning Joe Banks of the Hare & Hounds in St Giles, known as the Holy Land, and without doubt the most dangerous slum in London – would be the biggest man in the community, even if that community were largely a criminal one. His pub might be a lumber (a criminal rendezvous); he himself might be a fence (receiver of stolen goods), a smasher (distributor of counterfeit coins), or even a layer-on (heist organiser).

The fancy – the habitués of bare-knuckle prize-fighting outlawed in

Above The whitebait season – Gustave Doré's famous sketch of The Ship at Greenwich

the 1860s – were very much inhabitants of the pub world. Tom Cribb, on retiring from the ring, was set up as landlord of the Union in Panton Street, Haymarket (the pub now bears his name), by admirers who included Lord Byron. At such low haunts as Jem Burns's Queen's Head in Windmill Street and Sambo Sutton's Black Bull in Drury Lane, young swells could hire gloves and spar a few rounds with some old pug. Burns was also a noted fight promoter, being one of the backers of Tom Bendigo, who defeated Ben Caunt (himself landlord of the Coach & Horses in St Martin's Lane) for the championship in 1845.

Not all pubs warranted the suspicion of the genteel. In respectable suburbs and the quiet cul-de-sacs of the more select areas, restrained and well-run establishments entertained the servants of the upper and middle classes and the menfolk of those classes themselves (working-class women were seen in pubs, but never middle- or upper-class women).

Many landlords, too, were intelligent and high-minded men who actively fostered the growing political consciousness of their working-class customers. Working men's benevolent and friendly associations often had their bases in the upstairs room of a pub. London's coster-mongers (fruit and veg. barrow traders), for instance, whom the social commentator Henry Mayhew found to be republicans, socialists and "Chartists to a man", set up a friendly society known as the House of Lords at the Roebuck, Holborn; the Street Mechanics', Labourers' and Hawkers' Association had its home at the Lamb nearby.

Many pubs became "houses of call", hostels and employment exchanges for itinerant craftsmen, offering credit, hiring out tools and helping set men who were down on their luck back on their feet. A house of call would usually cater for one specific trade, often inventing an ironical badge of fictitious nobility to identify itself – hence the many Carpenter's Arms, Builder's Arms, Bricklayer's Arms and so on that dot the city.

But it is the gin-palaces which are the most solid legacy of the Victorian pub trade. Originally, these palaces of the poor were the distillers' answer to the threat posed by the Beer Act: to hit back at the new alehouses, many of which were no more than front parlours, they went to the other extreme. Extravagant opulence, they reasoned, would prove an irresistible lure to people whose own surroundings were so miserable, and they spared no expense in creating an illusion of luxury. Indeed, many of the most lavish of the gin-palaces were to be found in the worst slums.

The first gin-palace is generally reckoned to have been Thompson & Fearon's, opened in 1831 in Holborn Hill and usually attributed to the architect J B Papworth, who borrowed his design from current shopfitting fashions. All over London, new shop-fronts of ornately carved wood and brilliantly lit plate glass had sprung up – like a contagious disease, said Dickens; and where draper and grocers led, publicans were not far behind.

Within a few years, the term gin-palace was no longer applied merely to ornate dram shops, but to all pubs of a particular level of architecture and decor. Over the years, builders and designers borrowed a range of exterior styles from William & Mary to Swiss chalet to Renaissance Italian and eventually to a chaotic mix of them all; and all the while London's pubs grew larger and larger and more and more overblown.

Inside, the decor reached astral heights of fantasy which owed much to the march of technology. Perhaps the most important ingredient was the combination of gaslight and plate glass: carefully-placed mirrors and sheets of plate, breaking and reflecting the blaze of gas-jets, could make a small bar seem much larger.

The earliest methods of decorating plate glass were grinding and acid-etching, but after the 1840s new techniques made possible great panels of rich ornamentation. The most favoured decorative motifs were taken from nature: vine, hop and acanthus foliage, the national flowers of the four countries of the United Kingdom, birds perched on branches. In later years it became possible to achieve different depths of cut, which meant that several tones could be used to break up the light still further.

The glass revolution had an effect on beer itself. Previously, as beer had been drunk out of pewter or pottery, its appearance had hardly mattered. As glass became more common, drinkers came to prefer clear amber

Burton-style pale ale to dark, murky porter. By the end of the century, porter had lost its hold, sinking from around three-quarters to a quarter of all beer sold. Bottled beers, too, became more prevalent, and the old practice of taking a jug down to the pub to be filled became less common.

The original gin-palaces tended to comprise one room with little or no seating, where food was not sold, and where off-sales were as important as on-sales. Soon, however, the preference for separate rooms usual in old-style coaching inns and chop-houses crept back, and partitions of

Above Classic late-Victorian etched glass at The Bunch of Grapes

cut-glass and mahogany were everywhere installed. In time the different bars – saloon, public, smoking-room and so on – came to be grouped round an island or waggon bar forming a horseshoe or even a complete circle. A plethora of small rooms was often favoured: the Dun Cow in the Old Kent Road had no fewer than 11, and in some surviving Victorian pubs there are still little rooms which will seat only six or eight customers.

The counter itself was often a solid slab of mahogany, often with 'snob-screens' of louvered opaque glass at eye-level so that respectable drinkers need not fear being recognised. Backfittings became more and more elaborate, culminating in confections of highly-polished pillars, pediments and pinnacles like dream castles. The woodwork, generally oak, mahogany and rosewood and often artificially grained, was hand-made and as much a product of traditional craftsmanship as any medieval choirstall or hammerbeam roof. Wallpaper may have been acceptable in suburban saloons, but more favoured were moulded wall and ceiling-.coverings such as Lyncrusta, made of canvas and linseed pulp, Cameoid, or pressed paper, and Anaglypta, made of pressed paper pulp. These were the only examples of ersatz then in common use, and were meant to replicate hand-moulded plaster.

The era of the gin-palace came to a spectacular end in the last two years of the century. With reforming magistrates trying to reduce the number of licences and Burton brewers moving into the London pub market – competing for sites with London's own brewers and a substantial number of private owners – there was a scramble to attract custom by refurbishing the pubs in ever more opulent styles, with expense no object.

The 1890s saw a tremendous boom in pub building and rebuilding, followed almost immediately by an almighty crash as proprietors found that the returns did not repay the expense. Private owners went bust in droves – Frank Crocker of Crocker's Folly in Maida Vale (qv) was one such: the railway story is a charming piece of apocrypha – and even big breweries went through a five-year dry patch of no profits and no dividends. It was also a period of reform, when temperance was a political force: it was felt that the gin-palaces, for all their triumphs of design, were no more than cleverly baited traps for the vulnerable, who had to be protected by their moral betters from their own worst instincts.

It was at this stage that Olde English styles, both Gothic and rustic, came onto the pub scene, recalling sturdy yeoman virtues and echoing both the Pre-Raphaelite love of High Medieval and the preference of architects like Norman Shaw for a more vernacular idiom. This is the style that has prevailed ever since: other cities have large numbers of 1920s and 30s pubs inspired by expressionism, by classicism, by anything but Olde English; but London has few of these so-called improved pubs.

More recently, a confused attempt at the Victorian idiom has returned. There are a few frankly modern pubs such as Doggett's Coat & Badge, an outstandingly successful design; but by and large new pubs are decked out in a cliché of bare floorboards, bare brick walls, stained woodwork, shelves lined with books bought in car boot sales, and bric-à-brac bought wholesale. They fail because the depth of craftsmanship is seldom there: the Chandos in St Martin's Lane is a rare exception.

Worse still is the grim tide of theme pubs currently engulfing the capital. While researching this book I was stunned and speechless to find that Grafton's in Strutton Ground, Victoria, an old haunt with a rich history, had become a mock-Irish pub. The same fate has befallen the King & Keys, the old Daily Telegraph local in Fleet Street, and the Sun in Lamb's Conduit Street, Holborn, a cradle of the real ale revival in the 1970s. Perhaps the themers should look back 100 years and ask whether spending so much in pursuit of a shrinking market is really wise.

VISITING THE PUBS

Not so long ago, every pub bore the name of a brewery, and sold only that brewery's beers. This comforting certainty has, praise be, been largely blasted away by legislative change and corporate merger in the last decade. **Young's** pubs sell Young's beers, **Fuller's** pubs sell Fuller's beers and **Sam Smith's** pubs sell Sam Smith's beer; but they are the exception. **Bass** pubs will sell Young's, Fuller's and other independent brewers' ales as well the its own range of Bass, Stone's and Worthington. Guest beers are no longer a novelty and can be found, in addition to the house choice, in many of the capital's pubs.

ScottishCourage's ale portfolio includes such old brewery names as Younger's, Theakston's, Courage and John Smith's. **Carlsberg-Tetley's** includes Tetley and Ind Coope. The **Whitbread** range includes Boddington and Flowers. There is now a richer choice and profusion of beers in London than at any time since the 1930s: when in doubt, order a half of bitter.

It's not only the brewing scene which has undergone massive upheavals in the last decade: licensing law and pub etiquette have, too. Two bastions of pub history in particular have almost vanished: buying a round and afternoon closing.

Beer is now so expensive that the kitty system has all but replaced the old habit of buying rounds, and barstaff are used to being asked for an empty glass. The new system is less friendly, but has almost made extinct that stock figure, the expert at ducking his round.

Afternoon opening has been legal since 1988, and almost all London pubs, especially in the centre, exploit the new permitted hours of 11am-11pm Monday-Saturday. Sunday afternoon opening became legal only in 1995, and many pubs – maybe most – still take a well-earned break from 3-7pm. All in all, Sunday afternoon is a bad time to go pub-hunting: even many of those which declare themselves open all permitted hours actually take the Sunday break, so be warned. Enjoy London's pubs; but if you're visiting from abroad, here's one last vital tip: if you take a seat and wait for a waiter, you'll wait an awful long time!

THE
RIVERSIDE

The river has long been London's under-loved glory. For centuries

it was an industrial sump full of pollution, the reviled palace of

King Cholera. Then when London's docks died in the 1960s and

70s, the river fell into dereliction. Only in the Thatcher years, of

Yuppie urban living, did the Thames reawaken.

D ocklands became Wharfland, home of the luxury converted warehouse apartment. Among the warehouses – some original, some newly built – ancient pubs stand as they have done for three centuries, but prized today as they have not been for many years.

There is another river. In its western reaches the Thames is home to the Boat Race, to ancient palaces, and to grand pubs. Further west still it is almost rustic, with modest little pubs of unimaginable charm gazing into the dark water. This chapter covers a more dispersed area of the capital than any of the others; and for that reason the pubs are not listed alphabetically but in little itineraries which can be followed easily with comfy shoes, an A-Z, plenty of cash, and no appointments for the day.

Left The Prospect of Whitby at low tide viewed from the Thames

THE WHITE SWAN

THE RIVERSIDE, TWICKENHAM, TW9

In such a wealthy quarter, what a surprise it is to stumble across a little country pub. But then one remembers that this whole area was developed in early Georgian times to create a *rus in urbe*, a garden suburb of great mansions such as Orleans House and Marble Hill and the scarcely more modest houses of Lebanon Park and Sion Road, all set in leafy winding lanes, where figures of court and city such as Alexander Pope and Horace Walpole could fancy themselves country gentlemen. Clearly, a pretty little rustic inn was an essential accessory.

Certainly the White Swan fits the bill admirably. A white-painted cottage of about 1700, its plain front is broken up by balconies and stairs and a great bay beside the front door, big enough to be a snug in its own right. Inside there is one large, plain bar with lots of dark wood and nicotine plaster, and another room at the back where you will find the most stupendous buffet, a monumental cold roast joint or home-cured ham forming a mighty centrepiece.

The White Swan is a find in itself, but what really marks it out is its setting on a particularly beautiful stretch of the Thames. It has a riverside terrace facing Eel Pie Island a few yards across the water, all wooded and secluded, with little motor-launches bobbing at anchor. It seems incredible that Richmond Road is scarcely two hundred yards away.

Dickens was an admirer of the area: in a letter to Leigh Hunt he recalls visiting an alehouse that was actually on Eel Pie Island and had "a queer, cool, odd kind of smell ... suggestive of porter and pipes."

A fine way to visit – and an advisable one, thanks to the lack of parking – is on foot. It's now possible to walk the riverside from Richmond to Teddington, and the White Swan is handily placed for a halfway pint.

OPEN *all permitted hours*
STATION *Twickenham BR*
BEERS *ScottishCourage range*
FOOD *meals & snacks lunchtime & evening*

WHITE CROSS HOTEL
CHOLMONDELY WALK, RIVERSIDE, RICHMOND TW9

This handsome early Victorian Palladian-style double-fronted pub is one of a number of fine classical facades lining the Thames by Richmond Bridge – and is the only "real" one, in that Heron Court and the buildings grouped around it are actually the work of the modern neo-classicist and favourite of Prince Charles, Quinlan Terry, and conceal modern office-blocks.

The White Cross dates to an earlier outbreak of neo-classicism. It was built in 1835 on the site of a medieval house of Observant Friars, from whose badge it takes its name. However, the good friars would probably not have been too pleased with the hotel's raison d'être: dancing.

Formal dances were enormously popular with the middle and upper classes of the 18th and 19th centuries: indeed, it may be no exaggeration to say that, with the urban middle classes – who did not hunt and to whom the theatre was a touch racy – dances were the single most popular form of entertainment. Many towns had public assembly rooms where dances were held, and all towns had hotels with assembly rooms or ballrooms.

When the White Cross was built Richmond was a fast-growing suburb, still physically separate from London but economically and socially bound to it by the newly-built London & South-Western Railway. The White Cross served a burgeoning middle-class and served it well, its big, elegant ballroom (now a functions room) being

additionally blessed with romantic views of the Thames. How many proposals, one wonders, have been made and accepted on its small balcony between waltzes?

Today the White Cross is no longer a hotel, but it remains one of the popular pubs on this stretch of the Thames, especially in summer. Its front garden has a fashionably continental feel thanks to the beach-bar style hole-in-the-wall servery; pleasure boats depart for Kingston and Hampton Court from the pier outside; walkers out exploring the riverside mingle with shoppers and office workers; in the evenings the garden is lit with fairy-lights and a harpist plays from the balcony. It's not deserted in winter, though: in the bars three log fires blaze – one of them unusually located right under a window – while the policy of never buying in frozen or pre-cooked food, but always cooking everything from fresh, ensures a steady dining trade. Even the threat of flooding does nothing to diminish its popularity: if anything, it enhances it, since there's always the prospect of an inescapable lock-in.

OPEN *all permitted hours*
STATION *Richmond BR*
BEERS *Young's range plus guests*
FOOD *meals & snacks lunchtime*
Restaurant
Garden

THE CITY BARGE

27 STRAND-ON-THE-GREEN, W4.

Strand-on-the-Green is a long, narrow, pretty street which has attracted many artistic and literary residents – John Zoffany, Nancy Mitford and Dylan Thomas among them. There is no green any more – it was built on in the 1880s – but there is a strand in the form of a half-mile riverfront, and there are also three very fine pubs: the Bull's Head, the Bell & Crown, and the quaintest of them, the City Barge.

The pub claims to date from 1484, when it was the Navigators Arms. Until recently there was a "charter" of Elizabeth I hanging on the wall, which was stolen. It would be interesting to see this "charter", since ale-houses required a licence, not a charter, following Acts of Henry VII and Edward VI; and it's unlikely that licences were issued as such: when records of grants were kept, it was on a roll at the issuing court. If the thief would just fax the stolen charter back to the pub, the mystery might be cleared up.

With charter or without, the Navigators Arms carried on its business of keeping the folk of Chiswick in ale, but at some point, probably in 1618, when the Elector Palatine Frederick V seized the throne of Bohemia, changed its name to the Bohemia Head. Frederick was a popular hero in England not only because he was young, brave and Protestant but also because he was married to James I's beautiful daughter Elizabeth.

It remained the Bohemia Head until 1788, when it took its present name from the fact that the Lord Mayor of London's ceremonial barge was laid up every year for the winter nearby.

At this time Strand-on-the-Green, or plain Strand Green as it was then, was a straggling hamlet tagged on to the end of Brentford, probably looking much as it does now. It's a fair bet that the City Barge has changed little since then: it's definitely a country pub with its small, cosy, low-ceilinged rooms, its high-backed settles, its nicotine patina, and its cottage grate.

Which is ironic, really, seeing that the place was bombed almost flat in the war and was lovingly and faithfully restored by its then owner, Courage. The only give-away is that the quarry-tile floor is suspiciously unworn.

The biggest change since then has been the incorporation of the house next door as the New Bar (the old bar is called the Old Bar). This is a slightly plusher affair, where there is a restaurant and a conservatory.

The pub opens on to a Thames-side path which is regularly awash, hence the formidable steel flood-door protecting the Old Bar. Hence also the lack of a cellar; so when in the Beatles filmed a scene from *Help* at the City Barge in which Ringo appears to be falling into the cellar, it's a cinematic trompe l'oeil which was finished in the studio.

OPEN *all permitted hours*
STATION *Kew Bridge BR*
BEERS *ScottishCourage range*
FOOD *meals & snacks lunchtime & evening*

THE DUKE'S HEAD
8 LOWER RICHMOND RD, PUTNEY, SW15

It may seem strange to describe a pub as having been built purely for pleasure, since surely all pubs were. But the Duke's Head and its less well-preserved neighbour, the Star & Garter, never had any other function: they weren't community pubs, since the tiny community of Putney had, in the early 19th century, no need of great barrack-like boozers gazing over the river. They didn't serve a market: there wasn't one. They didn't serve old local wiseacres – and would probably have thrown them out if they had come in.

No, the Duke's Head and its neighbour were there because the Thames was there; and in particular because the Thames Regatta was there, and from 1854 the annual Oxford & Cambridge Boat Race was there too.

The Duke's Head was one of the earliest Young's pubs, having been acquired in 1832 shortly after the family bought the brewery. It was intended to serve not locals – although there is and probably always has been a street-facing public bar – but Londoners down for a day out in the country, Putney being a small town surrounded by fields until the 1880s.

In the 19th century it was always overshadowed somewhat by the Star & Garter, which was more closely connected with the Boat Race proper: the Duke's Head could only boast that it let the riverward side of its cellars as a boathouse to the local rowing club, while the Star & Garter was where the Oxford and Cambridge eights actually stayed in the run-up to the race.

Both pubs were given makeovers amounting virtually to a ground-up rebuild in the 1890s, the Duke's Head in

1894 and the Star & Garter about five years later. At the time Putney was growing considerably, although even in the early 1900s it still had a definable green belt. But the race was on to catch a year-round dining trade for the great riverside rooms, and the elegance with which the Duke's Head was redesigned in noble mahogany and swirling etched glass speaks loudly of the amount of money Young's was prepared to spend on winning.

How the owner of the Star & Garter responded is no longer evident, so drastic have successive refurbishments been; but it was grand enough to have been cited as an example in the advertising material of the glasswork company Cakebread Robey of Stoke Newington.

In recent years the Star & Garter has had money spent on it, but unwisely, while the Duke's Head is slightly faded, slightly scruffy even, but grand, like an aristocratic great-aunt. The riverside saloon has had the partitions which once divided it removed, but to the good: a riverfront room must be open to let in the soft reflected light from the water. To experience this effect, visit when the boat race isn't being rowed.

OPEN *11.30-3, 5-11 mon-fri, 11-11 sat-sun*
STATION *Putney BR, Putney Bridge tube*
BEERS *Young's range plus guests*
FOOD *meals & snacks lunchtime & evening*

THE DOVE
19 UPPER MALL, W6

Reached from Ravenscourt Park tube after a crossing of the busy Great West Road, the Dove is the centrepiece of a tightly-packed cluster of 17th and 18th-century houses which, until surprisingly late in the last century, provided the very affluent with a near-rural retreat which was still handy for the city.

Among the first of the district's wealthy residents, supposedly, was Charles II's neglected queen, Catherine of Braganza. It is also said that Charles himself used to slip out of an evening, when he was visiting her, to canoodle with Nell Gwynne here in the Dove. One wonders what he

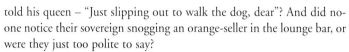

told his queen – "Just slipping out to walk the dog, dear"? And did no-one notice their sovereign snogging an orange-seller in the lounge bar, or were they just too polite to say?

Better attested residents of this charming little quarter were Dr John Radcliffe, the founder of the Hospital, Library, and Observatory of that name in Oxford, and James Thomson, the now-forgotten composer of Rule Britannia, who lodged upstairs at the pub and died of pneumonia in his room after taking his daily constitutional to Kew, getting caught in a downpour there, and hitching a lift back in an open boat.

Half of the old pub was bought by the brewer Fuller's – or Mawson's, as it then was – in 1796, probably at the same time as the other half was bought by the Duke of Sussex (Queen Victoria's uncle) as an out-of-town retreat. Queen Victoria's uncles were notorious libertines, so perhaps Sussex actually got up to what Charles II was only rumoured to have got up to.

Towards the end of the last century, London started encroaching on the Dove's little enclave, and the celebrities associated with the pub came down the social scale somewhat from royals and big landowners to mere literary types. William Morris lived next door, and Graham Greene and Ernest Hemingway were both frequent visitors. The pub appears, thinly disguised, as the Pigeons in A P Herbert's novel *The Water Gypsies*.

It is now one of the most popular pubs in the district, and deservedly so. It has a panelled snug which *The Guinness Book of Records* lists as the smallest in Britain at 4' 2" by 7' 10"; it has a cheery traditional bar with roaring fires in winter and walls covered in old prints; it has a dining room upstairs famous for its Thai food; it has a little terrace overlooking the river; and it has a conservatory almost covered by a great vine that actually bears grapes, although what variety I cannot say: Chardonnay, I hope.

OPEN *all permitted hours*
STATION *Hammersmith tube*
BEERS *Fuller's range*
FOOD *meals & snacks lunchtime & evening*

THE KINGS HEAD & EIGHT BELLS
50 CHEYNE WALK, SW3

Whether the Kings Head & Eight Bells really counts as a riverside pub is debatable. In recent years engineering works have "moved" the Thames several hundred yards so that the Embankment Gardens and the thundering A3212 now intervene. But, as the nautical second component in the name betrays, it was once. (Eight Bells is the traditional five o'clock call for sailors to reboard their ships.)

The pub you see now is a comfortable early Victorian affair – maybe a little older – with unusual large sash windows. It was remodelled in the 1880s or 90s, from which some glasswork survives, and was again refurbished in the 1960s (and not entirely unsympathetically). However, its pedigree goes back rather further than that: it is first recorded in 1580 when two licences (licensing by the local justices had been introduced in 1552) were merged. This was not at all an unusual practice and led to some interesting couplings which bar-room antiquarians to this day love to unravel.

The Five Bells & Bladebone in Limehouse is one such: the story is that an old abattoir was excavated under the Five Bells during building work, and a bladebone was kept as a grisly souvenir. But then a similar story is told of a pub in Hackney, except that in this case the bone was left over from an old murder.

The much-disputed Cat & Fiddle, recorded from early Tudor times, could easily be another: there are plenty of pubs called the Cat and one or two called

the Fiddle; so why go to the trouble of making up convoluted explanations – except, that is, for the fun of it? Either way, the King's Head & Eight Bells led an unexciting life on a quiet stretch of the Thames until the early 19th century – about the time of its rebuilding, in fact – when it was discovered by the painter Turner. Subsequently it became a fashionable meeting place for artists including Whistler and Augustus John, and, of course, their Bohemian hangers-on. Cheyne Walk and the nearby Cheyne Row have long been the desireable place to live for London's literati too: from Thomas Carlyle, George Eliot and Dante Gabriel Rossetti in the mid 19th century to Hilaire Belloc, T S Eliot and Ian Fleming in the 20th.

There's nothing Bohemian or nautical about the pub today, but it is still a very pleasant place with a fine dining-room at the back and a nice line in Belgian beers.

OPEN *all permitted hours*
STATION *Sloane Square tube*
BEERS *Whitbread range*
FOOD *meals & snacks lunchtime & evening*
Restaurant

MORPETH ARMS

58 MILLBANK, SW1

The very existence of Pimlico is a testament to the skill of one of the greatest engineers of the 19th century, a man whose name should rank alongside those of Metcalfe, Macadam and even Telford in the pantheon of diggers and delvers: Thomas Cubitt. If there had been no Cubitt, the Duke of Westminster would not today be the richest man in Britain; for it was Cubitt who, in the 1820s, worked out how to drain the swamps of south-west London which comprised the ducal estate, and which now includes some of the world's most expensive residential quarters.

Cubitt's next project was to drain the delta of the Tyburn, along the Thames to the south of Westminster Abbey; a work which was followed by the destruction of one of London's worst rookeries, the Devil's Acre, and the building of the broad-avenued Pimlico we know today.

The Morpeth Arms, a small but perfectly-formed gin-palace which retains much of its original mahogany and glass, was built in 1845 on land cleared by Cubitt for Paul Dangerfield, a publican-turned-spec builder whose first project had been the Lowndes Arms in Belgravia, also on land cleared by Cubitt, in 1829.

Dangerfield worked closely with his brother William: they tended to run the pubs they had built for a while before selling them, and while Paul was building the Morpeth Arms in partnership with a local builder, William was building up trade at the previous project, the Perseverance (now the gallery) in nearby Lupus Street. The Dangerfields were evidently a masterful pair: a letter from a foreman to his colleagues survives, warning against tampering with Paul and William's sister.

In its early days the Morpeth Arms had an impressive but gloomy neighbour in the form of the Millbank Penitentiary, a prison designed in the early years of the century by the philosopher Jeremy Bentham (whose mummified body – really – can be seen in the main hall at University College, London) which set the pattern for British prison-building for 150 years.

Bentham's innovation, which he called the Panopticon consisted of eight cell-blocks all radiating from a central tower, so all the blocks could be monitored from a single position. Millbank Penitentiary frowned down on the Thames until 1890, when it was demolished. Proposals for the site included a giant gas-holder; fortunately sugar millionaire Henry Tate's plan to build a gallery of modern art won. The Morpeth is now its local, and is the perfect place to reflect on Fauvists, pre-Raphaelites, Expressionists, Cubists and even piles of bricks (it was by Carl Andre and was called Equivalent VIII) over a nerve-soothing pint of RamRod or two.

OPEN *all permitted hours*
STATION *Pimlico tube*
BEERS *Young's range*
FOOD *meals & snacks lunchtime & evening*
Restaurant

DOGGETT'S COAT & BADGE

1 BLACKFRIARS BRIDGE, SE1

A pub which has just celebrated its 21st birthday, the Doggett's Coat & Badge is a kind of viewing platform from which a broad swathe of London's history may be seen. If you can get invited to a function in the pub's top-floor suite (or tip-toe up there anyway), take some time out on the terrace and scan the view from Parliament down to your left, across to St Paul's and the City to your right, and finally craning out to get a glimpse of the Tower of London.

It's a view which pretty much sums up London's history up to the Great Fire of 1666: Whitehall and the Tower, twin seats of royal authority, struggling vainly to hem in the aggressive ambition of the City's mercantile and political classes; the Tower slowly reduced first to a cypher, then to a curio; Whitehall itself lost as the centre of the royal authority and becoming the seat of the world's first modern Parliament. What a pageant to summon up in a single 90-degree arc of horizon!

If you are lucky enough to be here in mid-July, you will see another historical pageant, but a real, not an imaginary, one. The pub's curious name relates to a single-scull race inaugurated at a nervous moment in Britain's political history.

Thomas Doggett was an Irishman who became a successful theatre manager in the reign of William III (1688-1702). Being Irish at a time when the ousted Catholic Stuarts were making strenuous military efforts to regain the throne, he felt it necessary to be more Whiggish than the Whigs; on the accession of the fiercely Protestant Hanoverian George I in 1715, he felt a symbolic act to reinforce his loyalty was called for.

His brainwave was to inaugurate a race for six young and lusty Thames watermen from London Bridge to Chelsea Bridge, to be rowed on the anniversary of the Hanoverian accession every year, the prize being a coat bearing George I's badge (a white horse) and the word "Liberty".

The race has been rowed every year since then, having been won by eight members of the Phelps family in 1884, 1919, 1922, 1923, 1928, 1930, 1933, and 1938. The riverside patio of the ground-floor wine-bar at this eponymous pub is a good place to watch it from.

Doggett's Coat & Badge may only have been built in 1976, but it's a fine pub for all that. Unlike many new conversions of old buildings, it only nods in the direction of the past, rather than making the full prostration. Its four floors – wine-bar, bar, restaurant, and suite with terrace – are all comfortable, handsome, and spacious and all face in the right direction: the river.

OPEN *11-11 mon-fri*
STATION *Waterloo BR & tube or Blackfriars tube*
BEERS *Carslberg-Tetley range plus guests*
FOOD *meals & snacks lunchtime*
Riverside terrace

THE ANCHOR
1 BANKSIDE, SE1

Fire plays a large part in the history of the Anchor, for all that it stands by the river. It has been rebuilt twice after devastating fires, in 1750 and 1876; but it is most famous as the place from which a weary and disconsolate Samuel Pepys watched the Great Fire of London in 1666. Having taken a boat to observe the fire's progress, he wrote: "All over the Thames with one's face in the wind you were almost burnt with a shower of fire drops. When we could endure no more upon the water, we (repaired) to a little alehouse on bankside and there watched the fire grow."

The conflagration itself he described as: "one entire arch of fire above a mile long, the churches, houses and all on fire at once, a horrid noise the flames made, and the cracking of houses at their ruin." At that time the Anchor was already old, having been one of the countless low taverns in the unregulated stews of Tudor Southwark. It was the local for the Bear Garden, and Shakespeare's own Globe, now rebuilt, is scarcely 200 yards away.

Two centuries after Shakespeare's day, the Anchor was a home from home for Dr Johnson. He was a great friend of the Thrale family, who owned the nearby Anchor brewery until they sold it to Barclay, Perkins in 1781. Johnson had a room at the brewery where he could work on his dictionary in peace, and would repair to the tavern with Henry Thrale and such acquaintances as Oliver Goldsmith and David Garrick.

There his favourite beverage was a strong porter brewed by Thrale's for the Baltic trade, which survives today as Russian Imperial Stout, and which tends to support a new and wholly convincing theory that porter was named not after the market porters who allegedly favoured it, but after the export trade for which it was brewed.

After Johnson's day, the Anchor languished somewhat as an unpretentious beerhouse for the dockers and warehousemen of the district. So little was it regarded that it would have been demolished as part of a redevelopment scheme had not World War II intervened.

In recent years the whole area has revived, with ancient warehouses

'I took my wife & son to Bankside in Southwark where we Behold the whole city in dreadful flames near the Waterside' *John Evelyn Sept. 1666*

being turned into the luxurious flats and offices of Wharfland, and places like the Anchor with its nicotine-coloured plasterwork, black oak by the cubic metre, and warren of tiny rooms are considered a great asset.

OPEN *all permitted hours*
STATION *London Bridge BR & tube*
BEERS *Bass, Flowers, Greenalls Original, Greene King IPA*
FOOD *meals & snacks lunchtime*
Garden & riverside terrace

OLD THAMESIDE INN
2 CLINK ST, SE1

Thameside this pub may be; old it certainly isn't – not as a pub, at any rate. In fact it is one of a growing number of conversions from older premises which are rapidly transforming Wharfland into a pub-crawler's paradise.

Pickford's Wharf had, in its heyday, been a spice warehouse, but by the time the developers got their hands on it in 1985 – early on in the massive and still incomplete transformation of London's riverfront – it was derelict.

The quality was there, though. The masonry was sound; the great timbers were still in place; and the space was big enough and flexible enough to house a whole range of offices, shops and other uses, including this Nicholson's Inn.

Inside it's big but broken up into pleasantly intimate spaces, with a fine terrace overlooking the Thames, giving a grand view of Fishmonger's Hall opposite. The atmosphere is subdued without being over formal: waiters and bar-staff in black pinnies add gravitas, and there are newspapers provided so lone drinkers can browse unmolested.

Half of the pub's appeal is its location on the Riverside Walk between London Bridge and Cannon Street. Nearby are the Clink Prison Museum, Southwark Cathedral, and the Old Operating Theatre and Herb Garret museums at St Thomas's Hospital.

In a creek beside the pub, an old schooner named the Katherine & May used to be moored. It is gone now, replaced by a replica of the tiny ship in which the Elizabethan adventurer Sir Francis Drake circumnavigated the globe, the Golden Hind – named for the crest of his patron, Sir Christopher Hatton. It hardly seems possible to have achieved such great feats in such a small ship: perhaps that explains why Drake became slightly unhinged during the voyage and had his best friend, Thomas Doughty, executed for a fictitious mutiny.

OPEN *11-11 mon-fri, 11-5 sat, 12-3 sun (closed bank hols)*
STATION *London Bridge BR & tube*
BEERS *Carlsberg-Tetley range plus guests including locally-brewed Bishop's*
FOOD *meals & snacks lunchtime*

THE ANGEL
101 BERMONDSEY WALL EAST, SE16

The Angel is a very upmarket pub for surroundings that can at best described as workaday: an early 19th-century riverside inn set amid an early 20th-century estate of public housing – and thereby hangs a tale. The site has been an inn since the early 16th century, when it was built by the monks of Bermondsey Abbey, shortly before its dissolution. Opposite are the remains of a moated manor of

Edward III, one of a number of royal manors along the river.

A century later, the Angel is reputed to have been one of the places where Christopher Jones recruited hands and laid in stores for the voyage of the Mayflower and its landing of Pilgrim Fathers. Pubs often served this purpose, as readers of *Treasure Island* will know.

In the 18th century, Bermondsey was still a pleasant place of resort just outside London proper. Pepys was a frequent visitor to the Angel, ostensibly buying fruit from the neighbouring Cherry Gardens and taking curative waters at a nearby chalybeate spring – but actually visiting a lover, a Mrs Bagwell.

But as London spread, the area gradually declined, until in Dickens's day it had become one of the worst slums in London - "Jacob's Island, surrounded by a muddy ditch once called Mill Pond, but known these days as Folly Ditch ... Crazy wooden galleries with holes from which to look out on the slime beneath; windows broken and patched ... rooms so small, so filthy, so confined ... dirt-besmeared walls and decaying foundations; every repulsive lineament of poverty, every loathsome indication of filth, rot and garbage: all these ornament the banks of Folly Ditch."

It was this "filthiest, strangest, most extraordinary of the many localities which are hidden in London" that Dickens chose as the setting for the awful end of Bill Sykes in *Oliver Twist*.

All of this was thankfully swept away, except the Angel, and replaced with the neat and spacious estates which characterise the area today.

The pub itself is imposing and airy, opened up inside but still pleasantly sub-divided by railings, with one area raised, and plenty of old oak on view. The panorama of the City is as stunning from inside as it is from the riverside terrace.

OPEN *11-3, 5.30-11 mon-sat, 12-3, 7-10.30 sun*
STATION *Rotherhithe tube*
BEERS *Greenalls plus guests*
FOOD *meals & snacks lunchtime & evening – book for restaurant*

THE MAYFLOWER
117 ROTHERHITHE ST, SE16

Tucked between two converted warehouses on the Rotherhithe Walk, the Mayflower is one of those delicious survivals which transport one far away from modern London.

Its high-backed settles, big black oak beams, low ceilings and tiny rooms speak of long ago: on a slow day, when there's no-one there but you, your pint, and your imagination, you can see in your mind's eye the Pilgrim Fathers and their families filing anxiously but hopefully aboard the little Mayflower on their flight from religious persecution.

For this is the very spot from which the Mayflower is said to have set sail that day in 1620, returning eight months later to rot on the quayside when its captain, Christopher Jones, took ill and died. (He is buried in the churchyard of the elegant St Mary's just opposite, which was designed by John James, a pupil of Wren.)

The pub was called the Ship then, and so it remained for another century or so, until it was completely rebuilt at or soon after the turn of the 17th century, to be renamed the Spreadeagle & Crown. And there it stood, pretty much unchanged except for the addition of a mid-Victorian mansard roof, as a docker's pub in an unremarkable working-class area, surrounded by warehouses and wharves.

What tended to happen to pubs like this in the 1950s and 60s was that they were either torn down or, at best, modernised beyond recognition. Fortunately, the unique qualities of this particular pub were recognised by someone with the clout and the imagination to make something of them. Thus it was carefully restored, its olde-worlde charm skilfully retained, and renamed the Mayflower in 1957 in honour of the defining moment in its past.

A remarkable feature of this ancient pub is its own wharf, built out on piles over the river and commodious enough for 20 or 30 drinkers, provided they're not too heavy. The turbulent Thames is visible between the deck-planking, and although the neighbouring warehouses (which

credit themselves as among the first residential conversions in Wharfland) crowd in too close to allow much of a river view, it's a remarkably atmospheric place to spend an afternoon of ruminative bibulosity. Indeed, the only thing which is hard to imagine here is that 40 years ago London had dozens of pubs like this.

OPEN *11.30-11 mon-sat, 12-3 sun*
STATION *Rotherhithe tube*
BEERS *Greene King*
FOOD *meals & snacks lunchtime & evening*
Garden

THE TRAFALGAR TAVERN
6 PARK ROW, GREENWICH, SE10

One of the aristocrats of London pubs, the Trafalgar Tavern was designed and built in 1837 in grand Regency style, complete with great bow windows and wrought-iron balconies, by Joseph Kay, surveyor of Greenwich Hospital. It replaced an earlier alehouse, the George, a humble clapboard affair, and unlikely as it may seem, its construction was a venture dedicated almost entirely – in summer at least – to one commodity: whitebait, the fry of herring.

Greenwich in the 19th century was famous for its prodigious whitebait dinners, which were held between May and August, when the fish were hauled from the river in stupendous quantities. Even more curious, these were largely political affairs, with the Liberals holding their whitebait dinner at the Trafalgar and the Conservatives holding theirs at its deadly rival, the now-demolished Ship.

They came about simply because a member of Pitt's Cabinet used to invite his colleagues to his house on the river for dinner when Parliament rose for the summer, which coincided with the beginning of the whitebait season. These dinners soon outgrew his house and moved into the taverns, and when he died they were carried on.

At their height they attracted hundreds, who came to Greenwich by rail, by coach, and, in Gladstone's case, by Ordnance barge. An engraving in Doré's London Pilgrimage of 1872 shows the balconies of the Ship packed with wealthy revellers enjoying the summery evening. Others were less kind: Punch bitterly satirised the amount that was drunk at these events.

The great and good – Dickens, Wilkie Collins, Macaulay and Thackeray among them – continued to come until quite suddenly in the 1890s, when they died out almost overnight, unable to face the competition from the growing number of London restaurants. The Ship went bust and closed in 1908; the Trafalgar Tavern followed in 1915, and was turned into a seaman's rest, then a workingmen's club.

It was rescued in 1965 by Watney's, which reopened it with a design and execution which won a Civic Trust award in 1967. The atmosphere is much calmer and more restrained than it would have been before 1915: then, it was a riot of late Victorian carved mahogany and engraved glass; now, it has a classic coolness to it owing more to the 18th century than the 19th; its bars and dining room could be those of a rather good country hotel. As well as the ground-floor rooms – two parlours, a bar with seascapes, carved fireplaces and ornate plaster cornices, and a great dining room lined with photographs of visiting celebrities from Erica Roe to Norman Tebbit – there are a number of big function rooms upstairs, including the Nelson Room which has eight chandeliers.

Despite all this grandeur, the Trafalgar is most definitely a pub, not a restaurant: you can eat your whitebait with your fingers.

OPEN *all permitted hours*
STATION *Maze Hill or Greenwich BR*
BEERS *ScottishCourage range*
FOOD *meals & snacks lunchtime & evening*
Restaurant

THE CUTTY SARK TAVERN
6 BALLAST QUAY, GREENWICH, SE10

The old Union Tavern changed its name to the Cutty Sark in 1954 as a gimmick, to try and attract some of the tourists coming to see the 19th-century tea-clipper newly laid-up in dry dock and opened to the public. Not that Ballast Quay is all that near the centre of Greenwich where the dry dock is; in fact you have to pass the Naval Hospital, then the Trafalgar Tavern, then a pretty little pub called the Yacht, then the 17th-century almshouses now known as Trinity Hospital, then the hulk of Greenwich Power Station, before you reach it.

It's worth the trip. Part of a row of an attractive early 19th-century enclave of fine town-houses, which includes a harbourmaster's office, the Cutty Sark's true age is said to be at least a century greater. One clue may lie in the name: many pubs called the Union belong to 1707, the year of the Act of Union between England and Scotland.

The date of construction often cited is 1804, and the frontage, with its huge bow window curving elegantly out of the upper floors, is certainly late Georgian. Inside, though, it becomes evident from the low ceilings that the pub is, indeed, much older and has merely been refaced.

The decorative scheme, too, has an early 18th-century flavour, with bare floorboards, a mantelpiece fashioned from a seamed and worn ship's timber, lots of dark wooden boarding lining the walls, brass lanterns, coils of ropes, tables and chairs fashioned from barrels, and nautical pictures.

Up the great staircase which dominates the bar is a more comfortable, modern lounge with window-seats which command a sweeping view of this admittedly industrialised stretch of the Thames. A small and pleasant waterside terrace just across the sett-paved street has the same view.

The industry doesn't jar with the area's past, though: it's always been a working landscape. The very name of the street recalls an activity which was scarcely idyllic: Ballast Quay was where Blackheath gravel, quarried less than a mile away, was loaded for export to the Continent.

OPEN *all permitted hours*
STATION *Greenwich BR*
BEERS *Bass range*
FOOD *meals lunchtime, snacks lunchtime & evening Dining room upstairs Family room Garden*

TOWN OF RAMSGATE
62 WAPPING HIGH ST, E1

The Town of Ramsgate's thunder is always being stolen by its neighbours. There's the Prospect of Whitby claiming that Judge Jeffries was captured in its cellar (trying to flee the 1688 coup that unseated James II), when in fact he was apprehended on Wapping Old Steps right by the Town of Ramsgate. Then there's the brand-new Captain Kidd pub claiming to have been the site of Execution Dock, when in fact it was much closer to the Town of Ramsgate.

Why doesn't the Town of Ramsgate shout louder about itself? It certainly has the antiquity: in its earlier incarnation as the Red Cow it was already standing when the pleasant merchants' houses surrounding it were built in the early 18th century.

This redevelopment came shortly after the most notorious event in the life of Execution Dock: Captain Kidd went to his death there on May 22

1701; unjustly, many said. He was a commissioned privateer, not a pirate; the prizes he took were French, and we were at war with France at the time.

His real crime was to have cheated his aristocratic patrons out of some of the booty, and it was they who made sure that he hanged, even though they had to have him tried by Parliament (where he didn't help himself by appearing drunk); even though the ship carrying him from America to England was disabled in a storm and had to turn back; and even though the first rope on which he was hanged broke, throwing him to the ground. But there was to be no reprieve. It's a myth, incidentally, that the boat-borne river-pirates who would burgle ships at anchor while their crews caroused ashore, used to be tied to posts and simply left to drown: they were hanged first, then gibbeted in chains until three tides had washed over them, which is quite nasty enough without wishing it worse.

The cellars of the Red Cow were the setting for more grisly scenes: they were used as holding cells for press-ganged men waiting to board their ships, and for transportees awaiting their one-way voyages to America and, later, Australia. All that has been exorcised now. In fact the western end of Wapping High Street – unlike the eastern end, where Wharfland is a-building – is a delightful early Georgian enclave of prosperous merchants' houses and warehouses. The Town of Ramsgate, renamed after the Kentish fishermen who used to land their catch on Wapping Stairs, is an appropriately pleasant pub, long, narrow, wood-panelled and rather plusher than the other Thames pubs.

At the rear is a wooden deck overhanging the river, rather overshadowed by Olivers Wharf, an early warehouse conversion, on one side. And just in case all this pleasantness leads you to forget Captain Kidd and his luckless kind, there's a mock gallows complete with noose.

OPEN *all permitted hours*
STATION *Wapping tube*
BEERS *Bass range*
FOOD *meals & snacks lunchtime & evening*
Riverside terrace

PROSPECT OF WHITBY
57 WAPPING WALL, E1

Despite losing out to the Grapes as the most widely-accepted original for the Six Jolly Fellowship Porters in Dickens's *Our Mutual Friend*, the Prospect of Whitby is still the boss pub on this stretch of the Thames, just as the Anchor reigns on the opposite bank.

As well as being the biggest, it's also the oldest, with a date of origin of about 1520, and in its early days had a reputation for low villainy. Despite being surrounded by market gardens, its habitués were supposedly the riff-raff of the river, and the pub was named the Devil's Tavern in recognition.

A 17th-century habitué with a suitably diabolic legend to his name was Judge Jeffries, the hanging judge who presided over the gruesome aftermath of the Monmouth Rebellion of 1685, sentencing rebels to hanging, transportation or the lash by the dozen and accepting a peerage as first (and last) Baron Wem from a grateful James II. When James was overthrown in 1688 Jeffries tried to follow him into exile but was recognised, disguised as a coal-heaver – according to Prospect of Whitby mythology, in the coal cellar of this very pub – and carried off to the Tower, where he died soon after.

The legend has it that when he lived in Butcher Row off the Ratcliffe Highway he would dine on the balcony at the Devil's Tavern whenever there had been an execution, gloating over the remains. What spoils the story is that Execution Dock was hard by the Town of Ramsgate in Wapping High Street, and quite invisible from the Prospect of Whitby.

It's more likely that the official Judge's Lodgings were in Butcher Row and the Assize Dinners were at the Tavern, these institutions being the normal way of catering for the travelling judges who presided over the Quarter Sessions.

If Jeffries really did frequent the Devil's Tavern he would have bumped into Pepys, whose job as Charles II's Secretary to the Admiralty brought him here frequently. A coastal chart presented to him in 1686 is displayed in the Pepys Room upstairs, where the Pepys Society used to meet.

In the 18th century the old Devil's Tavern was burnt down and rebuilt as the Prospect of Whitby, taking the name from a coaster whose London moorings were nearby. In a politer age it became a pub for stevedores and other workers on the Thames; but the opening of a good restaurant upstairs in the 1950s drove it sharply upmarket: Princess Margaret, Prince Rainier and Kirk Douglas all dined here, and in 1953 the guests at a smart dinner-party were robbed of their jewels and cash at gunpoint by one Scarface Sanders.

Today it's a fine place from which to watch the river flow, with a stone-flagged public bar with its unusual pewter bar-top, a comfortable riverside lounge, a slightly raised dining area with wide views, and both garden and small terrace overlooking the Thames. The decor is all dark wood and the ambience is 18th century: if Pepys were to return, one suspects he might feel comfortable here – Judge Jeffries perhaps less so.

OPEN *11.30-3 5.30-11 mon-sat,*
12-3 7-10.30 sun
STATION *Wapping tube*
BEERS *ScottishCourage range*
FOOD *meals & snacks lunchtime & evening*
Restaurant, Garden

The Grapes
76 NARROW ST, E14

There is great argument among tap-room intellectuals as to whether Dickens based the Six Jolly Fellowship Porters in *Our Mutual Friends* on the Grapes or the Prospect of Whitby just upriver. It's generally considered that, as the Grapes is in Limehouse, the Grapes has it, although the pub Dickens describes seems far larger than today's long, narrow two-bar tavern: maybe it's a composite; or more likely the Porters is, like the Maypole in *Barnaby Rudge*, a meringue of artistic imagination founded on the thinnest possible biscuit-base of actuality. On one point the Grapes and the Porters agree: like the latter, the former is: "long settled down into a state of hale infirmity. In its whole constitution it had not a straight floor and hardly a straight line; but it had outlasted and would yet outlast many a sprucer public house."

(Mind you, if it looked like that in Dickens's day it can't have been very sturdily built, since it dates only to 1720, along with its neighbours replacing a group of late Tudor buildings lost in a fire.) The Grapes that Dickens knew – and know it he did, having been obliged as a child to get up on a table here and sing for the company – was in many respects a low beerhouse, where watermen were liable to row drunks out into the Thames, drown them, and sell the cadavers for dissection.

But pass through into the snug overlooking the river, and one would find a cheery scene where Bob the potboy was busy making the hot purl – porter, sweetened and spiced, heated in an iron funnel thrust into the fire, and finally fortified with gin -which gave the Porters its nickname, the Early Purl House. Hot drinks of all sorts figure large in the work of Dickens and his contemporaries, who valued the companionable

theatricals of making them up as much as they enjoyed the finished result. It's a shame they've died out. In Dickens's day, and up to the 1960s, this was a working landscape and the Grapes was a working-class pub. In the front bar there hangs an oil by Alice West, painted in 1949, portraying the Grapes and its regulars.

But paralysis and ruin gradually overcame London's Docklands, and by the late 1970s the area was virtually derelict. In the 1980s, the creation of Wharfland had begun. The work has been seemingly endless, and where the builders could not find a real warehouse to convert into luxury flats they build replicas with varying degrees of ineptitude. Occasionally one sees characters out of the West painting wandering the streets with a haunted expression: they must be former residents on a sentimental return journey, because they certainly couldn't afford to live here now. Whatever one thinks of the gentrification of Limehouse, it has breathed new life into this ancient gem of a tavern with its plain bareboard public bar, its cheerful little riverside snug, its tiny gallery overhanging the river, and its outstanding fish restaurant upstairs. A classic.

OPEN *12-3, 5.30-11 mon-fri 12-3, 7-11 sat, 12-3, 7-10.30 sun*
STATION *West Ferry DLR*
BEERS *Carlsberg-Tetley range*
FOOD *meals & snacks lunchtime & evening*
Restaurant

THE CITY & EAST END

It may be hard to summon up the London of Donne and Pepys,

Dickens and Johnson from the concrete canyons of today's City

Yet dive down any alley and it's there. True, the ancient buildings

were all swept away in the Great Fire of 1666.

But behind the main thoroughfares the cluttered street-plan and the zesty mercantile culture survived, and the flavour has been unmistakably preserved in confections such as the incomparable Jamaica Wine House and Ye Olde Cheshire Cheese.

Linking the City to Westminster was Fleet Street, which became a natural home for the newspaper industry – keeping an ear on both the political and financial worlds. And as you can imagine, with so many journalists to cater for, the street is home to many fine inns.

To the east, in the shadow of the Tower, lay the villages – Whitechapel, Stepney, Bethnal, Bow – which made the East End of ill fame. At Aldgate and Liverpool Street the stiff-collared City merged into the terrifying, murky underworld of Jack the Ripper.

Left The Viaduct Tavern in the shadow of the Old Bailey

THE BLACKFRIAR
174 QUEEN VICTORIA ST, EC4

This curiously-shaped pub was built on an awkward corner site in 1875, taking its name from the Dominican convent founded here in 1278. It was, for 30-odd years, a perfectly ordinary pub belonging to a licensee named Pettit. But in 1902 or thereabouts he let Henry Poole get his hands on it. Poole was a leading figure in the Arts & Crafts movement founded by William Morris and the like — artists and writers with a penchant for the Arthurian — and was, in fact, master of the Art Worker's Guild in 1906.

He was chosen for the job in the context of an Edwardian revulsion against the marbled grandeur of the 1880s and 90s, and its retreat to a cosy yeoman myth of medieval or Tudor imaginings. This was the England of Lutyens, of whole suburban streets of villas with fake half-timbering nailed to their gables; and in pub design there was a conscious move away from the degeneracy of the 90s towards something older, purer, more manly: the mock-medieval Cittie of York, the Lyceum, the George, and the Coal Hole, all in the Strand, Ye Olde Cock in Fleet Street ... and this.

"By jumping a matter of three centuries," say Gorham & Dunnett, "they resurrected the idea of the traditional English inn which at that time was being rediscovered and endowed with ye olde halo."

But the Blackfriar is different from all its contemporaries in that it is perhaps the only building in Britain – possibly in the world – whose entire decorative scheme flows from a basis of arch flippancy and self-conscious facetiousness.

Its exterior is laden with bronze plaques of fat jolly friars (a theme invented, says Girouard, "by the late 19th-century Academicians to titillate their Protestant buyers") symbolising the pleasures of drink; they reappear inside, in bronze and terracotta, but against a background of the most gorgeous veined and striated marble columns and bands; of gilt mosaic; of glittering mirrors.

The craftsmanship is awesome; but the whole place is an elaborate joke – a fact borne out by the deliberately trite aphorisms carved around the walls of the back snug or grotto: "Industry is All"; "Wisdom is Rare"; "Silence is Golden" – if one of them said "You don't have to be mad to work here, but it helps", you would not be surprised.

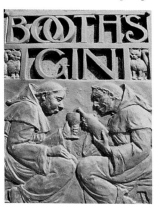

Despite a certain lack of seriousness, the Blackfriar is still undoubtedly one of London's treasures, and in its way a landmark in British art history.

OPEN *11-11 mon-fri, closed sat-sun*
STATION *Blackfriars tube*
BEERS *Carlsberg-Tetley range plus guests*
FOOD *meals & snacks lunchtime only*

THE BLIND BEGGAR
337 WHITECHAPEL RD, E1

Of course George Cornell, a member of the South London Richardson gang, shouldn't really have been drinking in the East End – and he certainly shouldn't have called Ronnie Kray, the East End's top gangster, "a fat poof". But on 8 March 1966, he was in the East End, in this very pub; and on that night this pub became famous.

Cornell's reaction when Ronnie confronted him that night was to sneer: "Well well, look who's here." Ronnie preferred action to words: he raised his 9 mm and shot Cornell in the eye. He was later to taunt twin brother Reggie into the equally-celebrated murder of another gangster, Jack "The Hat" McVitie. It was the Krays' undoing: on the fourth anniversary of the shooting of George Cornell, they went down for life, and British gangsterism on the American pattern went with them.

Since then the Blind Beggar has done its best to mop up the blood. A big late-Victorian pub on the outside, on the inside every trace of its past except the lincrusta ceiling has been ruthlessly expunged.

Instead of the warren of little snugs and bars the Krays knew, there is one huge horseshoe-shaped room, gorgeously bedecked with red-shaded wall-lights, leather sofas and armchairs, gingham bistro table-cloths in the dining area and modern brick fireplaces. There is even a conservatory. The whole resembles nothing so much as the lobby of a conference centre in a modern seaside resort.

And yet, even as the shade of Jack the Ripper stalks the skyscrapers of Bishopsgate, so Cornell's blood will always be a faint brown stain on the rich red carpets of today's Blind Beggar.

One romantic and enduring thing about the Blind Beggar is its name. This relates to a story told about both Harold, the last Saxon King, and Henry, the son of Simon de Montfort. Both died in battle; both were reputedly "seen" years later wandering blind as mendicants by followers who could not come to terms with their deaths. The Blind Beggar of Bethnal Green is the title of a 16th-century ballad and a 17th-century

drama on the theme.

Next door is the remnant of the old Mann Crossman & Paulin brewery, outside which General Booth, founder of the Salvation Army, preached his first sermon in 1865. In 1958 it became part of the Watney empire of keg and lager infamy. Now Watney's, once as reviled as the Kray Gang, is just as dead and gone.

OPEN *all permitted hours*
STATION *Whitechapel tube*
BEERS *ScottishCourage range*
FOOD *meals & snacks lunchtime & evening*

Above The Blind Beggar – a shrine on the East End gangster trail

DIRTY DICK'S
202 BISHOPSGATE, EC2

The connection between this fine Young's pub with its restaurant and wine bar and the notorious recluse of Leadenhall Street is slight, but the pub has made a good living on the back of it for nearly two centuries.

Dirty Dick was the nickname given the unfortunate Nathaniel Bentley, a prosperous ironmonger and dandy who lived at 46 Leadenhall Street. Tragedy struck Bentley on the very day that he was to be married: all was ready for the service, and the wedding breakfast was laid out in his house, when Bentley's attractive and well-connected bride fell ill and died. Grief-stricken, Bentley locked up the room where the breakfast was to have been held and never entered it again.

As for his dandified appearance and fastidious ways, they too soon fell in desuetude. Seeing little point in living, Bentley certainly saw no point in washing, or changing his clothes, or cleaning his shop, or burying the bodies of his cats when they died; and soon he acquired the nickname by which he is remembered.

But fate has a fine sense of irony, and far from pining away as he surely wished, Bentley lived to a ripe old age; while his business, far from dying of neglect, acquired a reputation and flourished – to the point where, when Bentley finally retired in about 1814 (he died in 1819), the enterprising landlord of the otherwise unremarkable Old Port Wine House in Bishopsgate bought the entire contents, wedding breakfast, dead cats and all, and put them on display in his pub – renamed, naturally enough, Dirty Dick's – as a grisly attraction. (It certainly tickled Charles Dickens's fancy for the grotesque, inspiring his creation of Miss Haversham in Great Expectations.)

So potent a lure did this story prove that even when Dirty Dick's was pulled down in 1870, the exhibits were carefully dismantled and replaced in the new pub that was built on the site. In time, though, it was found that while horror may fascinate, it does nothing for the

appetite: drinkers were more repelled than attracted by the swags of cobweb and displays of dust-coated hardware, and in 1985 the whole lot was swept away with the exception of the odd mummified cat or two.

What remains is a very good example of a City pub-cum-wine bar with its bare floorboards, oak and glass screens, wooden panelling and exposed brickwork.

OPEN *11-11 mon-fri, closed sat, 12-3 sun*
STATION *Liverpool St BR & tube*
BEERS *Young's range*
FOOD *meals & snacks lunchtime*
Restaurant

HAMILTON HALL
LIVERPOOL STREET STATION, EC2

L ondon's mainline railway termini, and especially their attendant hotels, have in recent years provided an architectural treasure-trove almost as rich as the Pyramids of Egypt.

Built in an age of opulence and shuttered 40 years later in an age of austerity, their ballrooms and lobbies, their great stairs and saloons, have ever since been gathering dust, been preserved in dust, been pickled in dust, awaiting some cross between Midas and Schliemann to bring them back to life.

Such has been the fate of the Grand Ballroom of the Great Eastern Hotel at Liverpool Street Station. Built in 1901, it was the magnificent last efflorescence of an age already dying. Thirty or 40ft high, it was modelled on an appartement of the Palais Soubise, a Louis Quinze confection in Paris. That means blowsily sensuous nymphs and overmuscled predatory Greek gods which anyone of unrefined sensibilities might confuse for soft porn for the Classically-educated bourgeoisie.

It played host to dancing from that era to that of the Charleston in the 20s and beyond. Closed down initially for the duration of the Second World War, it was never resurrected during the cash-strapped post-war decades. The refurbishment of Liverpool Street in the 80s drew attention to the potential dormant in the ballroom, and its restoration was put out to tender. The J D Wetherspoon Organisation, a company specialising in making great pubs out of unpromising premises, won the bid, and let fly its painters and decorators.

The only change the firm has had to make, beyond freshening up those plaster extravagances with a lick of paint, has been to build a bar into one corner of the ballroom, with a mezzanine on top; but the place still feels like the ballroom it once was. The sensation is inescapable that if someone were only to strike up some Strauss, all those tired commuters and secretaries preparing for their nights out would suddenly start whirling in time.

OPEN *11-11 mon-sat,
12-3, 7-10.30 fri*
STATION *Liverpool St
BR & tube*
BEERS *range changes,
many guests*
FOOD *meals & snacks
available 11-10*

HOOP & GRAPES

47 ALDGATE HIGH ST, EC3

Described bluntly, the elements that give this ancient pub its persona — bare floorboards, planking dadoes, nicotine-coloured plaster — link it to the Lord Rodney's Head(qv)not three-quarters of a mile away in Whitechapel. But in character they are a thousand miles apart. For this is no working-class local which has miraculously survived the refurbisher's jackhammer, but a venerable gentleman of the pub scene.

It is in fact the only timber-framed building left in the City, having escaped the Great Fire of 1666 by a mere 50 yards. One of the first things the city fathers did, once the flames had sunk to embers, was to ban timber-framing as a means of construction; even the old Hoop & Grapes (then a vintner's) replaced its frontage with less combustible materials in about 1670: the carvings on the little stone gate-posts are crude enough to date from that rebuilding.

During the intervening centuries, the old building slowly and comfortably settled and sagged, as timber frames will. About 100 years ago it evolved from a wine-importer's depot into a pub; but not much else changed until the 1980s, when owner Bass all of a sudden noticed that the place was falling down. A £1.2 million rescue and refurbishment programme followed, during which the old Hoop & Grapes was underpinned and given a new steel skeleton. Well, the proof of the pudding is in the eating; and the Hoop & Grapes certainly has the flavour of authenticity. It's a big pub, but broken up by black wood

partitions into bite-sized spaces; there's a nice big front window to sit in and watch the suits from the City go by.

OPEN *11-11 mon-fri, closed sat, 12-3 sun*
STATION *Aldgate tube*
BEERS *Bass range plus Fuller's London Pride*
FOOD *snacks & meals lunchtime &*
evening

JAMAICA WINE HOUSE
ST MICHAEL'S ALLEY, CORNHILL, EC3

The acres between Cornhill and Lombard Street are truly remarkable in that the alleys, courts and entries actually retain the medieval street plan. This is common in England's cathedral cities and market towns, but almost unknown in the City itself, which has so often been razed and redrawn.

The Jamaica Wine House is to be found down a narrow alley on the south side of Cornhill and is one of a cluster of three old back-alley pubs which have made it through the hazards of the centuries: the 17th-century George & Vulture has medieval origins and figures in the *Pickwick Papers*; it is now a restaurant. Simpson's Tavern, built in 1757, is also mainly an eating house but does have a separate bar. But it is the Jamaica which has the story, for it was the first coffee-house in England.

Coffee was introduced by merchants returning from Turkey in the 1630s and 40s as a curiosity; one of them, a Mr Edwards, following the custom of the day, set up his faithful servant Pasqua Rosee, variously described as Greek, Levantine, or Armenian, in business on this site in 1652 by way of reward for years of faithful service.

A handbill of Rosee's, displayed in the ground-floor bar of the Jamaica, explains why coffee was such an instant success: "It prevents drowsiness and makes one fit for business if one has occasion to watch; and therefore you are not to drink it after supper unless you intend to be watchful, for it hinders sleep for three or four hours."

In those days, much commerce went on in taverns which sold only wine and beer; and understandably business became less crisp as the working day wore on. Here was the antidote: a drink which sharpened the wits, rather than dulled them. Despite all manner of reactionary blasts – including a poem containing the immortal couplet "English apes! Ye might, for aught I know/were it but mode, learn to eat spiders too!" – there were 3,000 coffee-houses in London by the turn of the century, including Lloyd's (the original home of Lloyd's of London).

Rosee's was replaced towards the end of the 19th century with today's extraordinary pub. With its bare boards and sombre mahogany partitions, the place really resembles the

sixth-form common-room of a particularly tradition-ridden minor public school. The clientele, all of whom are clearly engaged in one or other manifestation of money-juggling, fit the pattern admirably.

OPEN *11-11 mon-fri*
STATION *Bank tube*
BEERS *Whitbread range*
FOOD *meals & snacks lunchtime*

THE JERUSALEM TAVERN
BRITTON ST, EC1

The Jerusalem Tavern is a fine example of that not-unusual London phenomenon, the wandering pub. Throughout London's history it has been common for licensed victuallers, when moving pub, to take their old pub's name – and hopefully thereby, some of its custom – with them. Thus Ye Olde Cock in Fleet Street was on the other side of the road until 1887, and the Cittie of Yorke was Hennekey's until even more recently, "borrowing" its present name from a long-gone tavern in Staples Inn.

The Jerusalem Tavern, however, is more peripatetic than most. It is recorded as existing in the village of Clerkenwell, which had sprung up around the crusading Priory of St John of Jerusalem, as early as the 14th century.

A remnant of the Priory is St John's Gate, which dates from just before the Dissolution, and for centuries the Jerusalem Tavern actually occupied part of the gatehouse. One of the best-known coffee-houses of its day, it even gave its name to a quart-bottle the landlord favoured.

The original Jerusalem Tavern closed in about 1754, and the name attached to the Red Lion in what used to be Red Lion Street, now Britton Street, simply because the landlord used the same sort of bottle.

The new Jerusalem Tavern was a place of high reputation, attracting Dr Johnson and his circle and also providing a meeting-place for nascent friendly societies and trade associations, taking its place in Clerkenwell's tradition as a centre for working-class organisations of all descriptions. However in 1878 the tavern was pulled down to make way for what is now Clerkenwell Road.

Today's Jerusalem Tavern was built as a fine town-house in

1720; but the street was known mainly as a centre of the watchmaking trade, and most of the houses, including this one, were eventually turned into workshops. Its present front was added in 1810, and when it was bought by the newly-established St Peter's Brewery of Elmham, Suffolk as its first London pub, it had been a café for many years.

The Brewery and its award-winning architect were determined to recreate an early 18th-century coffee-house in the premises, and have gone to town with the bare boards, dark oak, and little rooms. Whether they have succeeded or not is for you to decide: you'd never guess it had only been a pub since 1996.

OPEN *all permitted hours*
STATION *Farringdon BR & tube*
BEERS *St Peter's range*
FOOD *meals & snacks lunchtime & evening; breakfast from 7.30 am*

LAMB TAVERN
LEADENHALL MARKET, EC3

Leadenhall Market was designed by Sir Horace Jones, also the architect of Billingsgate and Smithfield; and at one time Leadenhall rivalled them both in furnishing the burgeoning City with the thousands of tons of provisions it required each day.

The Lamb actually dates back to around 1780, when it was established by a wine-merchant named Pardy, but the W B Simpson tile picture in the lobby of Wren Inspecting Plans For the Monument dates the current tavern to a century later, when it became a famous City "stand-up"

boozer for male clientele. Here stockbrokers and market porters actually rubbed shoulders, given that time allowed for meals was short and workers of all classes had to grab what they could when they could.

Leadenhall, though, couldn't stand the pace on its cramped and inaccessible site, and was one of the first City markets to capitulate to the developers. Today it is frankly kitsch: the ceramic fruits that decorate it are suspiciously freshly-painted; it smells not of carcasses but of gentlemen's cologne; and anyone not wearing a suit is not a porter but a tourist.

Still, the Lamb Tavern retains its raison d'être: Lloyd's is hard by, and the number of financial services workers within a quarter-mile radius is as uncountable as the sands of the desert, and they all want a lunchtime drink, and most of them seem to want it – and why not? – right here. The Lamb Tavern has grown to accommodate them: not outwards, because it can't, but inwards, with the insertion of a mezzanine reached by a spiral stair, increasing the number of trading floors from three (including the dive-bar in the cellar) to four. The top-floor bar was the first in the City to go smoke-free: eat there, if you want to taste your food. Not all the customers are bankers: John Wayne, Robert Mitchum and Tom Selleck have all filmed here.

OPEN *11-10 mon-fri, closed sat-sun*
STATION *Fenchurch St, Bank & Monument tubes*
BEERS *Young's range*
FOOD *meals & snacks lunchtime*

THE LORD RODNEY'S HEAD
285 WHITECHAPEL RD, E1

Scarcely quarter of a mile from the chicken-in-a-basket plush of the Blind Beggar, the Lord Rodney's Head(qv)could scarcely be more different. Indeed, if asked which of the two had been the scene of a gangland murder, you might well make the wrong guess.

But there's something honest about the Lord Rodney's Head, and none of the flash that would have attracted the East End's Capone-worshipping racketeers of the 1950s and 60s. A long, narrow pub with the bar stretching down one side, its plain matchboard walls, bare floorboards and rickety bentwood chairs could equally well have been installed in 1900 or 1860 or even 1782, the year of the Battle of the Saints in which Admiral Rodney crushed the French navy and became both a household name and the adornment of many a pub-sign.

If there is another pub in the East End as basic as this, it is well hidden. The Lord Rodney's Head doesn't make it into many guidebooks, but if you want to step straight into the past, don't miss it. It's authentic right down to the street-traders' cries drifting in from the market-stalls outside and the handful of cheese rolls under a glass dome on the bar.

Once there were scores of East End pubs just like this; descendants in style of the basic one-room dram-shops of the late 18th and early 19th centuries, where drink was taken fast (or bought by the jug to take home) and refinements were thought

unnecessary. But all of these old pubs had their peculiarity, their homely touch, their signature, and in the Lord Rodney's Head's case the peculiarity is mantelpiece clocks, over 100 of them, lining the picture-rail shelf. There's still room for more: if you want to curry favour, visit a house-clearance shop before you visit the pub and pick up a present for the collection.

Opposite is the London Hospital, once the refuge of the Elephant Man. If you see, through a slight fog, a figure in bowler and ulster hurrying by, it's not the ghost of Sherlock Holmes but that of Sir Frederick Treves, surgeon and philanthropist, on a mission of mercy to the teeming poor of the district.

OPEN *all permitted hours*
STATION *Whitechapel tube*
BEERS *Banks & Taylor range, traditional cider*
No food

THE OLD BELL,
95 FLEET ST, EC4

I t may seem callous to applaud a fellow human being's ruin, but if Henry and Richard Baker had not overreached themselves and gone dramatically bankrupt, we would probably not have this 17th-century gem today.

More than anyone else, the Baker Brothers epitomised both the pride which caused the great pub-building boom of the 1890s, and the fall which ended it.

Over a period of 20 years they built up an empire, buying, rebuilding, and as often as not selling on at a handsome profit. With their favoured architects, Saville & Martin, they bought and embellished many of London's greatest pubs: the Angel, Islington; Ye Olde Cock, Highbury Corner; the Horseshoe, Tottenham Court Road; the Punch Tavern, Fleet Street; the Tottenham, Oxford Street. At the same time, they bought a clutch of hotels and restaurants around Leicester Square.

But as the '90s wore on, business got harder. While the magistrates were trying to surpress "surplus" licences, rival brewers were competing for what was left, driving prices up. Decors became more and more elaborate – and expensive. And as Temperance crusades began to bite, people began to drink less.

The Bakers bought the Old Bell in 1897. The inn had been built in 1678 by Wren himself, for builders working on St Paul's, it is said – but then, it's also said of the Salutation, Newgate Street and the Old Watling, Bow Lane, so maybe it's true and maybe it isn't. There had probably been an inn on the site before the fire, variously named the 12 Bells, the Swan, and the Golden Bell, so perhaps its revival was merely part of the general process of regeneration, and perhaps Wren had nothing to do with it. But then again ...

It was only a small, simple pub – the front part had been a

wine and spirit merchant since the tax on wine was reduced in 1860, and that made it even smaller. The Bakers liked their pubs big and ornate – not many of them survive, but a quick look at the Tottenham will reveal what sort of pubs the Bakers favoured, and what they doubtless had in mind for the Old Bell.

But before the masons, the glaziers, the plasterers and the cabinet-makers could move in, the Bakers went spectacularly bust in the biggest, but not the only, business failure of its kind: poor Frank Crocker was contemplating his four-storey leap at about this time. And so the Old Bell was never rebuilt. Instead, it fell into the hands of Nicholson, the distiller, a major creditor of the Bakers, and thus in time to Allied Domecq, who restored it, taking out the Victorian wine merchants and returning the whole site to its wonted use as a tavern.

Today it is an unaffected, simple pub: dim and dark without being gloomy, full of black oak, broken up into cosy little nooks, with stone flags on the floor and a scuffed and comfortable mien.

OPEN *11-11 mon-fri*
STATION *Blackfriars tube*
BEERS *Carlsberg-Tetley range*
FOOD *meals & snacks lunchtime*

YE OLDE CHESHIRE CHEESE
WINE OFFICE COURT, 145 FLEET ST, EC4

Visitors who come to Fleet Street expecting to encounter the Dickensian London of mazy courts, crazy buildings, and deep, dark alleys populated by beer-sodden journalists and claret-swigging QCs are all too often disappointed by the workaday reality.

However, if they care to peer down an unprepossessing entry on the north side of the former Street of Shame, about halfway between Fetter Lane and Shoe Lane, they will find exactly what they were looking for. The Olde Cheshire Cheese in Wine Office Court (which was the home of the Royal Excise until the Great Fire of London; hence its name) is pretty plain from the outside, but to venture in is to knock 200 years off the tariff of time.

Here is precisely the warren of saloons and snugs that fantasy insists should comprise a 17th-century city tavern – six of them, in fact, along with three restaurants and a private dining room, and all complete with bare board floors (fresh sawdust twice daily), wooden settles (easy on the eye, not so easy on the bum), and ancient smoke-blackened oak beams.

The Cheshire Cheese was already just over 80 years old when the celebrated wit and lexicographer Dr Johnson moved into 17 Gough Square almost next door in 1748. It had been built in 1667 on the site of a medieval friary which had been swept away in the Great Fire the year before and whose vaults, including well and sewer, survive.

Oddly, it's just about the only pub which Johnson is not actually attested as having visited; but it was his local, so perhaps his forays there were too mundane for Boswell to record. At any rate, there is a chair there which the owners swear was his, and why not humour them?

Later literary visitors are better-attested: they include Thackeray and

Dickens (of course), who gave the Cheshire Cheese a name-check in *A Tale Of Two Cities*. In the 20th century the pub became even better-known: Chesterton and Belloc and Conan Doyle were frequent visitors. Another celebrity of the time was a parrot, Polly by name, of such longevity that its eventual demise was marked by a *Times* obituary.

OPEN *11-11 mon-sat, 12-3 sun*
STATION *Blackfriars tube*
BEERS *Sam Smith's range*
FOOD *meals & snacks lunchtime & evening*

YE OLDE COCK TAVERN
22 FLEET STREET, EC4

Not the original Cock Tavern, nor even the second Cock Tavern, the present holder of the name is the third, although you'd never know it to look at it.

The Cock was one of the great taverns of 17th- and 18th-century Fleet Street along with Nando's and the Mitre. A James I fireplace survived the conflagration of 1666, and its overmantel is always said to have started life as the inn's sign, carved by the hand of Grinling Gibbons himself. Pepys was a regular visitor, not least because the landlady of the time, a Mrs Knipps, was one of his many lovers.

Probably because of its location at the eastern end of Fleet Street – equally handy for journalists and, with the Temple next door and the Law Courts opposite, lawyers – the Olde Cock remained a prominent City tavern into the Victorian era. Dickens and Thackeray were visitors, and Tennyson penned possibly his worst piece of verse here:

"Oh plump head waiter at the Cock
To which I most resort,
How goes the time?
– Tis five o'clock.
– Go fetch a pint of port."

If he was drinking port by the pint, it's no surprise. But connections with Dickens and Tennyson, however revered they were, cut no ice with the property developers of the late

19th century, and in 1887 the Olde Cock shared the fate of many of its near-neighbours. Like the Mitre, which vanished under a branch of Hoare's Bank, the Olde Cock was demolished to make way for a branch of Coutt's. Unlike the Mitre, the Devil and others, though, the Olde Cock was rebuilt across the street, still with its James I fireplace and Gibbons overmantel, in a style appropriate to a replacement 17th-century tavern described by Marc Girouard as Old English or "back-to-the-inn".

"Their exteriors favoured roughcast and low eaves; their interiors looked clean and bright with plenty of scrubbed oak and exposed brickwork, oak settles in the inglenook, and Windsor chairs scattered across the tiled floors," says Girouard; but before you agree with him too enthusiastically, the Olde Cock you are seeing is not the same pub he saw in the early 1980s. In fact it was seriously damaged by a fire in April 1990, and the bar is a reconstruction (although the fireplace and overmantel seem to have escaped for a second time).

Although today's oak-rich bar with its wooden settles, antique-looking bar gantry, and glass screens is not strictly the Real McCoy, the careful restoration creates an atmosphere in which the scenes described in the Victorian magazine *Epicurean Almanack* do not seem alien:

"The back of the room is occupied by a knot of sages who admit strangers into their fraternity on being presented with a crown bowl of punch. Mine host used to smoke his pipe among them nightly. Marsh, the oyster-man, attends here the whole season with his natives, Miltons, and byfleets."

I'm not so sure about the knot of sages, who sound an infuriating crowd; but I wonder what became of Marsh?

OPEN *11-11 mon-fri*
STATION *Temple tube*
BEERS *ScottishCourage range*
FOOD *meals & snacks lunchtime only*
Restaurant

THE OLD DR BUTLER'S HEAD
MASON'S AVENUE, COLEMAN ST, EC2

It wasn't only Victorian nannies who held that if the medicine tasted nasty, it must be doing you good: the precept apparently also held good in the pre-enlightenment world of James I, and Dr William Butler was its chief apostle.

Dr Butler was in fact completely unqualified, but achieved fame with his quack would-be cures. He believed, for instance, that the best way to cure epilepsy was to make the sufferer jump: by which token he would creep up behind his patient and without warning fire off a brace of pistols. Similarly, his cure for the plague was to throw the shivering sufferer into a nice cold pond.

This logic clearly appealed to James I, also known as "the wisest fool in Christendom", who made Dr Butler court physician and, in order to compensate for the lack of letters after his favourite's name, wangled an honorary degree for him.

Dr Butler's most lucrative line was his very own brand of snake oil. Medicinal ale proceeded from the same curious principle as his other cures: that if you were ill, more of the same was bound to do you good. Medicinal ale was intended to cure digestive ailments, and was therefore flavoured with all sorts of stomach-turning nasty herbs.

The original hair of the dog, it was enormously successful among a credulous public, and Dr Butler was able to license it to a host of willing taverners. Franchisees advertised the fact by displaying his portrait as their sign (just as Kentucky Fried Chickens are identified by portraits of Colonel Sanders); this particular Dr Butler's Head, founded in 1616 and rebuilt after the Great Fire of 1666, is the last.

Like Dr Butler himself, it is not all it seems. It may look Jacobean, with its bare floorboards, dark wood settles, nicotine-coloured plaster and so forth; really it is a rebuilding of a rebuilding and in fact is a rather fine Victorian interpretation of the genre. Palaces of glass and marble were for the masses: Victorian City gents had been raised on Dickens

and Washington Irving and liked their pubs antique. (The fine half-timbered building opposite, by the way, is even less authentic: it was built in 1928.)

OPEN *11-11 mon-fri*
STATION *Moorgate tube*
BEERS *ScottishCourage range*
Restaurant

YE OLDE MITRE TAVERN
ELY COURT, OFF ELY PLACE, EC1

Finding the Olde Mitre is rather like stumbling across Narnia. Ely Court is far too insignificant to appear in the street maps; but should you find yourself admiring the diamonds in Hatton Garden's countless jewellers' shops, you might just stumble across one of its entrances.

Alternatively, should you find yourself in Charterhouse Street, you might just wander into the rather fine Georgian quadrant of Ely Place; and should you err into the insignificant alley leading to the left at the first lamp-post, you will be in Ely Court and, inevitably, in the Olde Mitre (it is the only building in Ely Court). The question is: will that magical lamp-post, that unremarkable entry, be there next time you pass?

Hard to find the Olde Mitre may be; little-known it most certainly is not, for it is one of London's most historic pubs. Ely Place is the site of the Bishop of Ely's palace, built in the late 13th century, and until very recently the quarter was a self-governing enclave of Cambridgeshire. It was one of London's great palaces, mentioned twice by Shakespeare (*Richard II*, Act I, Scene 1; *Richard III*, Act III, scene 4); John of Gaunt spent his declining years here after his great Savoy Palace was burnt down in the Peasant's Revolt; Henry VIII and Catherine of Aragon were entertained to a five-day banquet here in 1531.

The first Mitre was built in 1546 for the refreshment of palace servants and went through many vicissitudes, acting at different times as a prison and a hospital. As a memento of those times there is preserved in one of

the bars a fragment of cherry tree round which Elizabeth I danced the Maypole; the present building, though, dates only from 1772. (All that is left of the original palace is St Etheldreda's Chapel, given to the Spanish ambassador in 1620 and thus the first post-Reformation Catholic church in Britain.)

As for the pub itself, even to a visitor who knows nothing of all that weight of history (and there is more: it figured large in the love-affair between Elizabeth I and Sir Christopher Hatton, for instance) it has the charm of centuries upon it. Dark but not dingy, small but not poky, this is one of those rare places where an older London elbows its way into the modern world. Oh – and Dr Johnson drank here.

OPEN *11-10 mon-fri, closed sat, sun.*
STATION *Chancery Lane & Farringdon tubes*
BEERS *Carlsberg-Tetley range*
FOOD *snacks lunchtime & evening*

YE OLDE WATLING
WATLING STREET, EC4

Can this heavily-beamed City tavern be as old as it seems? It is so laden with oak beams that surely it must be ancient. Well, yes and no. Standing on the oldest city street in Britain, the pub is always claimed to have been built in 1668 by no less an architect than Wren himself, as a commissariat for workers building his new St Paul's, which looms majestically at the end of the street.

That precisely the same is said of the Old Bell in Fleet Street need not weaken either claim: it must take more than two pub-fuls of builders to put up a Cathedral, and anyway, there are Wren churches near both pubs, so perhaps the builders were actually building those and somewhere under a 1960s office-block there's a third, forgotten, Wren pub where the workers who built St Paul's actually lodged.

It's also said of the Olde Watling that it has a frame made of old ship's timbers. But while old ship's timbers really were used for building – having been pickled in brine for years, they were strong; they tended to be good straight lengths; and, being scrap, they were cheap – timber-framing was understandably banned in London after the fire, so that claim at least we can dispose of.

Having been sceptical about the Olde Watling's historical claims, there's no need to be sceptical about the Olde Watling itself. It says it was restored in 1901, and that is almost certainly the date of origin of the decorative scheme. We have early English-style flat-arched doorways; we have oak columns; we have matchboarding, panelling, exposed (or nailed on) crucks, ties, and transoms; we even have studded leather wallcoverings in parts.

All this speaks of the vogue for Olde English which followed the sudden collapse of the fashion for marble, ceramics and glass in 1899. It was a style which spoke of English medieval heroes,

manliness, chivalry, honour, opening doors for ladies, cricket and all the other virtues which champagne-swilling, actress-chasing Edwardian English gentlemen upheld in public. Like many City taverns, the atmosphere here is very mannish: the front bar has no tables or chairs, just a few bar-stools and a shelf round the wall. This is perpendicular-drinking territory: if you must sit, there's a dining room upstairs.

OPEN *11-11 mon-fri*
STATION *Mansion House tube*
BEERS *Bass range plus guests*
FOOD *meals & snacks lunchtime*
Restaurant

THE OLDE WINE SHADES
6 MARTIN LANE, OFF CANNON ST, EC4

The Olde Wine Shades is an infuriating place. For while it's so old that antiquity seems to hang like a haze about its timbers, it has no actual history. Built in 1663, the Olde Wine Shades somehow survived the Great Fire just as, even more miraculously, it has survived the intervening centuries, pretty much intact. It is the very model of a proper old city wine-bar: bare floorboards with a scrap of old carpet-runner as ancient as the oak; the ceiling striped with beams nearly 350 years old; high-backed settles making private compartments with ancient scrubbed-wood dining tables.

It's not hard to believe, this being the City, that not so very long ago a property development company proposed to demolish the place: one can only guess at how many such venerable places must have vanished in the last century. What beggars belief is that, in the face of indignant protests from City chaps who knew and loved the place, the developers proposed a compromise: they would encapsulate the Olde Wine Shades in the lobby of the glass behemoth they wanted to build.

Influence told: the property men were headed off; the Olde Wine Shades survived just as its regulars wished. The art of wielding power is to wield it effortlessly; the art of wearing wealth is to wear it lightly. The Olde Wine Shades fits these precepts like a glove – no not like a glove. Like a comfortable and well-worn old carpet-slipper.

OPEN *11-11 mon-fri*
STATION *Monument tube*
BEERS *drink the wine*
FOOD *meals & snacks 11.30-3*
Restaurant in basement
No jeans. Men must wear ties

THE VIADUCT TAVERN
126 NEWGATE ST, EC1

This handsome little corner-site pub of the 1870s stands on what must be one of the most melancholy sites in England: for this was once Newgate Prison, where public hangings were held. Little is left to remind the visitor of Newgate's grim existence, although it was London's most notorious prison from the middle ages until the late 1860s, when it was finally demolished and replaced by Holborn Viaduct.

One trace, perhaps, survives in the cellars of the Viaduct, where a small room is said once to have been a debtors' cell which held 16 offenders who begged for alms through air-holes which let out from the cell's ceiling through the pavement.

It seems an unlikely story, as debtors were rarely held in such horrible oubliettes and in fact were often lodged in apartments with their families around them (although Dickens, aged 11, had to provide for himself by working in a boot-blacking factory when his father was jailed for debt).

But George Theodore Wilkinson, in his Newgate Calendars, describes "two very close apartments ... one at the foot of the master's, another at the foot of the common side, which serve the purpose of chandler's shops by day and sleeping-rooms at night ... always too full; indeed it is difficult to conceive how the prisoners exist, crowded as they are, and breathing the same polluted air."

The ornate pub which replaced this hell-hole

could hardly be more wholesome, with its painted mirrors bearing scenes from Greek myth (a little soft porn, Victorian style), its intricately patterned ceiling, its brilliant-cut glass screens, grand marble dado, and mahogany bar-wagon.

But although the victims of justice are but a faint memory here, its executors are an ever-present fact: the Old Bailey is opposite, and lawyers are thirsty people.

OPEN *11-11 mon-fri, 12-3, 7-11 sat-sun*
STATION *St Paul's tube*
BEERS *Carlsberg-Tetley range*
FOOD *meals & snacks lunchtime & evening*

THE WIDOW'S SON
75 DEVONS RD, E3

This famous East End pub is also known as the Bun House, thanks to one of those poignant melodramas the Victorians loved so much and upon which there are innumerable minor variations. At some point during the Napoleonic Wars – or before, or shortly after – a young man went to sea, leaving his widowed mother to run the family beerhouse on her own, assuring the weeping relict he would be back by Easter, and exhorting her to be sure to keep a hot cross bun against his inevitable return.

Naturally, he never came back; and equally naturally, his mother failed to believe him lost, keeping his hot cross bun threaded through a string hanging from the ceiling and adding another every year pending his looked-for return – a custom maintained by subsequent landlords ever since.

A slight variation is that the widow was not a publican herself, but lived in a neighbouring cottage; and that her collection of mouldering hot-cross buns was bought at auction upon her death as a gimmick by a local publican, and added to every year thereafter.

Yet another slight variation has it that the custom died out in the early part of this century, that the collection of withering buns was largely if not wholly destroyed by wartime bombing, that the custom was revived after the last war, and that few if any of the buns now hung up in their string bag predate 1945.

Stories like this were meant to be enjoyed, not necessarily believed; and it's credible enough to persuade the Royal Navy to send a party with a new hot cross bun every Good Friday to be added to the collection at a 9 am church parade.

The pub itself has an exceptionally pretty frontage of

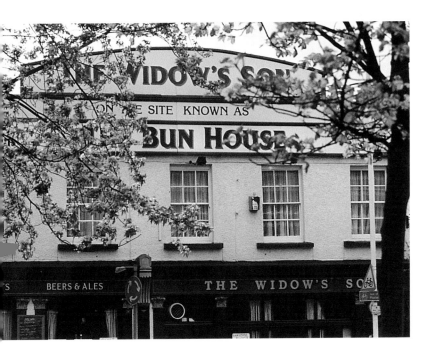

about 1850, kept lively with a profusion of hanging baskets, window boxes and so on. Inside, it has been pretty much stripped of anything original except perhaps the matchboarding which lines the walls and has been painted white to give a high, cool, airy feel. The area is fairly unprepossessing, but the pub is a jolly enough place, determinedly local despite the fame of its story.

OPEN *12-3, 4.30-11 mon-thur, 12-11 fri-sat, 12-4 , 7-10.30 sun*
STATION *Devons Rd BR*
BEERS *Carlsberg-Tetley range*
FOOD *meals & snacks lunchtime*
Garden

WILLIAMSON'S TAVERN
1-3 GROVELAND COURT, BOW LANE, EC4

Williamson's is one of those places which is pleasantly hard to find: Groveland Court does not even make it to the index of many London street-maps, but it exists, and is even reckoned to mark the precise centre of the City; and in it is Williamson's.

Some confusion surrounds the exact origins of the building depending on what you read: in the 15th century it was the site of the mansion either of Sir John Fastolf, the great commander of the later stages of the Hundred Years' War, or of Sir John Oldcastle, a Lollard burned for heresy; either way, Shakespeare's Falstaff is supposedly a conflation of the two.

Whosever house it was, it must have perished during the Great Fire of London – well, everything else did – and was replaced with a new residence for the Lord Mayor: the wrought-iron gates bearing the monogram WM were a gift from William and Mary (1688-1702).

By the 1730s, however, the premises were no longer considered gracious enough for the Lord Mayor, and in 1739, at the same time that today's Mansion House was commissioned, the old one was sold to Robert Williamson, who turned it into a hotel.

The hotel's first and longest-residing guest was none other than the Lord Mayor of London, since the architect Dance the Elder took until 1752 to complete the Mansion House.

It was evidently a popular hotel with middling sort of people – country businessmen, ship's captains, even bulb merchants from the Low Countries; but it hardly seems to have been opulent. For instance, oak beams were out of favour in the neo-classical 18th century: Mr Williamson's solution was not to plaster them over properly but to nail up cotton sheets and whitewash them in a cheap but highly inflammable imitation of plaster. In the 19th century matches were banned for fear of fire: smokers had to light their pipes with tapers supplied by the staff.

The last Williamson, James, died a wealthy man in 1914 and the hotel was auctioned. It was evidently still not all that opulent since a flyer of

1916 addresses itself to customers "who do not wish to pay for the glitter of gilt and brass buttons". By the 1930s, the old building was decaying. In 1934 it was rebuilt as a City tavern by a property developer named Hollis, who also built the office blocks next door and moved the wrought-iron gates from the Bow Lane end of Groveland Court to their current site.

The pub he built has all the virtues of the best of 1930s pub design; like the Freemason's Arms in Hampstead, its three large rooms are light,

airy and elegant: rather classier, if anything, than what they replaced.

OPEN *11.30-9 mon-fri*
STATION *Mansion House tube*
BEERS *Carlsberg-Tetley range plus guests*
FOOD *meals & snacks lunchtime. Restaurant*

HOLBORN, BLOOMSBURY & COVENT GARDEN

Holborn and Bloomsbury are the seat of intellectual London, where many of the capital's great institutions of learning are to be found. Bloomsbury, of course, became famous for the artists and writers who lived there in the first half of this century.

W hether Leonard and Virginia Woolf and the rest of the Bloomsbury Set were great users of pubs is not known; but the more bohemian types who gathered round Augustus John in the Fitzroy Tavern certainly were, as were BBC-patronised poets such as Louis McNiece and, of course, Dylan Thomas. But the area is not all rakehells and wastrels; it has many sober and dignified streets with pubs to match like the Lamb in Lamb's Conduit Street – untouched by time.

Between the Strand and St Martin's Lane is Covent Garden. Its famous piazza, once the home of a bustling market and its attendant street porters (notorious for sinking a drink or two) is now a busy tourist attraction with shops, street theatre and still the odd gem of a pub.

Opposite The Lamb and Flag in Covent Garden, once known as the Bucket of Blood

THE CHANDOS
29 ST MARTIN'S LANE, WC2

Big and dignified, the Chandos stands at the gateway to London's theatreland, and being surely the capital's best-located pub, it is consequently perhaps its most popular early-evening rendezvous as well.

It's a fine pub, its interior having won awards as a pioneering piece of design. For although the imposing exterior is late Victorian, the interior dates only to 1984 when Yorkshire brewer Sam Smith's bought the place and revamped it completely. To do justice to the pub's grandeur, the brewery designers chose to chuck out the tatty chintz of a slightly earlier vogue and go back to basics: hand-crafted high-quality joinery and tilework. Its bar, bare floorboards and intimate booths are all made to a standard of craftsmanship that would not have been out of place when the pub was first built.

Upstairs is the more comfortable Opera Room, which has a separate entrance and serves breakfasts from 9 am.

The pub is named after a Georgian scion of the Chandos dynasty, whose founder made his name and fortune as one of the most notorious English raiders in the latter part of the 100 Year's War. By the 1720s and 30s, however, his descendants in the Chandos clan, who were busily developing this corner of London, had become less bloodthirsty. In fact the particular Chandos after whom the pub is named was a great patron of Handel's.

OPEN *all permitted hours*
STATION *Charing Cross tube*
BEERS *Sam Smith's range*
FOOD *meals & snacks lunchtime & evening*

THE CITTIE OF YORKE
22 HIGH HOLBORN, WC2

A true aristocrat among London pubs, the Cittie of Yorke is the descendant of inns which have stood on the site since 1430, although the earliest surviving fabric belongs to 1645 or thereabouts, when it became the first of five Hennekey's wine-bars in London. The Cittie of York's great glory, however, is not its distant past but its fantasy-Gothic architecture, which is less than a century old.

The stone oriels on the frontage, and the magnificent Long Bar with its galleries, booths, medieval-style great window and high gantry – complete with vast wine-tuns that were drained in the blitz and never refilled – place the Cittie of Yorke firmly in the early years of this century, when pub architects revolted against the marble palaces of the 1890s such as the Princess Louise at the other end of High Holborn.

Instead, they looked back for their inspiration to a mythical Englishness rooted in Chaucer, Shakespeare, coaching inns, and Mr Pickwick – a style described by Marc Girouard as the "back-to-the-inn" movement, glorying in "half-timbered gables, leaded lights, bottle-glass, lanterns, wooden barrels, carved black oak, and artificially smoked ceilings between artificially warped beams" and described at the time as Mock-Antique.

In its various stages of debasement - and it has never really gone away – the Mock-Antique style has become worse than pastiche; for one thing later designers never take into account is that to take a space the size of the Long Bar and dress it up convincingly takes craftsmanship and money – in spades. Without them, you end up with a village hall with the 2x4 pine rafters painted black and the odd swirl of Artex here and there.

However, the Cittie of Yorke must be judged on its own terms, and as a mock-medieval spectacular, it works brilliantly. To quote Gorham & Dunnett, referring to an academic reconstruction of the Mermaid Tavern, Cornhill, as it was in about 1420: "Making due allowances for the changes of five centuries, this seems not at all unlike the Long Bar at

Hennekey's [as the Cittie of Yorke then was] in High Holborn.

"Take away the long bar counter and strew the floor with well-trodden rushes and you might well be going into a 15th-century tavern when you penetrate into that long high-raftered hall."

The pub's present name, incidentally, is as ancient as the pub, but it does not belong here. The Cittie of Yorke was long ago a pub in Staples Inn across the road. The present Cittie of Yorke was taken over with the rest of the Hennekey's chain by the Yorkshire brewer Sam Smith's in 1979. They liked the name, and promptly nicked it.

OPEN *11.30-11, 11.30-3, 5.30-11 sat closed sun*
STATION *Chancery Lane tube*
BEERS *Sam Smith's range*
FOOD *Meals & snacks lunchtime & evening*
      Restaurant

THE LAMB
LAMB'S CONDUIT ST, WC1

The Lamb is pleasantly located in an urbane side-street on the borders of Bloomsbury and Clerkenwell; the beers are Young's, and therefore good, and always kept in the condition Mr Young and his brothers would like; but most of all, it has one of the finest pub interiors in the capital.

The street owes its name to Sir William Lamb, a philanthropist who in 1577 not only built a conduit to bring clean water – a perennial need in a growing city – to the households of the quarter, but who also supplied 120 pails to the poorest householders to carry it in. The pub which bears his name is a good deal younger, being first reported in 1720 and still reminiscent of the period in its proportions, despite subsequent rebuildings.

Its interior and its glory, though, belong entirely to 1894 when, like so many old London inns, it was lavishly and expensively remodelled. And although the partitions which originally radiated out from the horseshoe-shaped bar have, as in nearly all cases, been removed, it still retains plenty of other features of the period.

Top of the list are its complete set of brilliant-cut glass pivoted snob-screens, arranged at face-height so that gentlemen who didn't want to be identified by the staff didn't have to be. This mania for privacy, even secrecy, seems strange to us, but judging by the number of snob-screens which have survived in pubs across Central London, it was the

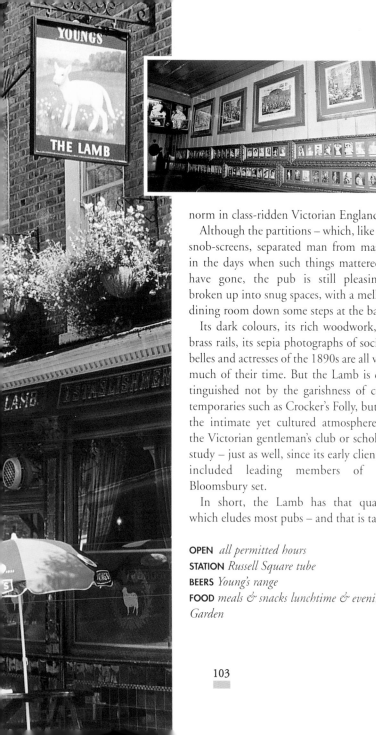

norm in class-ridden Victorian England.

Although the partitions – which, like the snob-screens, separated man from master in the days when such things mattered – have gone, the pub is still pleasingly broken up into snug spaces, with a mellow dining room down some steps at the back.

Its dark colours, its rich woodwork, its brass rails, its sepia photographs of society belles and actresses of the 1890s are all very much of their time. But the Lamb is distinguished not by the garishness of contemporaries such as Crocker's Folly, but by the intimate yet cultured atmosphere of the Victorian gentleman's club or scholar's study – just as well, since its early clientele included leading members of the Bloomsbury set.

In short, the Lamb has that quality which eludes most pubs – and that is taste.

OPEN *all permitted hours*
STATION *Russell Square tube*
BEERS *Young's range*
FOOD *meals & snacks lunchtime & evening*
Garden

LAMB & FLAG

33 ROSE ST, WC2

Perhaps London's oldest pub, the Lamb & Flag has been licensed since 1623 and the fabric of the building is said to be Tudor, although it's impossible to tell by looking. The pub was originally the Coopers Arms and stands in a street, then known as Red Rose Street, that was beyond the reach of the Great Fire of London in 1666.

It was never a particularly savoury area. The poet John Dryden was ambushed on 19 December 1679 in the alleyway beside the pub and beaten half to death by thugs supposedly hired by Charles II's current mistress, who was stung by Dryden's satirical versifications.

A little strange, since at the time Dryden was alternating between comedies of manners and works of Shakespeare-worship, and didn't publish his most biting satire against the court, *Absalom and Achitophel*, until 1681. So perhaps he was just the victim of a random mugging, or perhaps they were looking for fellow-satirist, Samuel Butler, who lived in Red Rose Street. At that time this was a fairly honest working-class area, "fit for mechanics and people of mean quality", but by the late 18th century it stood on the edge of the most festering, packed, squalid slum in central London, the Holy Land.

Even after the Metropolitan Police were founded in 1829, they could only make arrests in the Holy Land in large, heavily-armed squads with reinforcements close at hand; and that was with St Giles's Police Station nearby.

As if to rub in the message, the pub was at that time

known as the Bucket of Blood, supposedly because prize-fights were held there. In the late 1850s the area was largely redeveloped and became if not genteel at least honest, and the Cooper's Arms settled into a period of picturesque stability.

Its last remodelling occurred around the turn of the century, from when the fireplace and glass screens originate. Like the Lord Rodney's Head in Whitechapel, it has a reassuring working-class no-frills solidity about it – panelled dado, hessian wall-covering, built-in benches, bare floorboards, dark pressed-paper ceilings, all slightly scruffy.

It feels very real and has a vaguely 1950s ambience; and as it is off the main Covent Garden drags, it still attracts a sprinkling of real London characters.

OPEN *all permitted hours*
STATION *Covent Garden tube*
BEERS *ScottishCourage range*
FOOD *meals & snacks lunchtime*

MUSEUM TAVERN
49 GT RUSSELL ST, WC1

You need an appetite for hard work to be landlord of the Museum Tavern, for just across the street is one of the most powerful tourist attractions in Britain: the British Museum itself, whose queues of hungry and thirsty visitors guarantee that the Tavern needs never want for custom.

The pub owes everything to its premier location. Until 1823, when the Museum was built, it was the Dog & Duck, but it was quickly renamed in honour of the institution which made its fortune. It was rebuilt in 1855 to cope with the stream of visitors to the new attraction – they included Karl Marx – and is one of the few survivors of the work of architect William Finch Hill.

Hill was best-known as a designer of early music halls, of which there were many, in a style described by Marc Girouard as "the opulent but never licentious classicism" which prefigured the more exuberant and eclectic decorative schemes of the later Victorian years.

Many of the pubs he designed were actually attached to music-halls, although this is not one; he was one of the first pub architects to develop a distinct design personality, especially in his handling of interiors, which in the earliest gin-palaces had tended to be as bare as the exteriors were elaborate.

Outside, there are benches, tables, hanging

baskets, big gas-style lanterns, and all the other paraphernalia of the traditional Victorian pub.

But sadly, the four partitions with which Hill subdivided the bars are long gone, swept away to make room for the crush of Museum visitors; in fact nothing survives of Hill's interior save the elegant mahogany bar-back – and even there, the glass has all been replaced.

In the cyclical nature of things, the Museum Tavern's interior has reverted to the rather canteen-like appearance it must have had before he remodelled it. There is even a shortage of chairs, doubtless to allow more people in; and if Karl Marx, who refreshed himself often here between stints while researching and writing *Das Kapital* in the British Museum reading room, were to come back to Bloomsbury, he would find nowhere to sit.

OPEN *all permitted hours*
STATION *Russell Square tube*
BEERS *ScottishCourage range*
FOOD *meals & snacks lunchtime*

PRINCESS LOUISE
208 HIGH HOLBORN, WC1

One of London's truly great pubs, the Princess Louise languished until a few years ago as a dingy keg-only beerhouse, half-empty most of the time, its architectural splendour utterly neglected, cherished only by a handful of aficionados.

In fact it sank so far that in the sacrilegious 1970s Watney's actually proposed to pull it down; which actually turned out to be no bad thing in that it finally alerted the sleeping giant of public opinion to the dreadful carnage that was being wrought on London's built heritage – far worse than anything the Luftwaffe had achieved – and the ensuing uproar was an important step in raising public awareness of the need for conservation.

Today the Princess Louise, unexceptional from the street but a treasure-house inside, is one of the most admired pubs in the whole of Britain, and one which every visitor to the Capital should drink in.

The pub, which is named after Queen Victoria's fourth daughter, was actually built in 1872, and the original publican's office behind the long oval bar is a rare survival. Before the bar was built, customers were served by waiters, and this was where the beer was drawn.

The present decor dates to 1891 and was designed by an otherwise unknown architect, Arthur Chitty. As Marc Girouard points out, the contractors in this case, all highly esteemed and experienced practitioners, must have had as much influence as the architect; and if the Princess Louise is anything it is the climax of craftsmanship.

The glasswork (by R Morris & Sons of Kennington) and tiling (by Simpsons & Sons of St Martin's Lane, which provided pictorial panels for many great 90s pubs, nearly all of them gone) are unparalleled; every surface is profusely if not fantastically decorated; even the gents' loo is a treasure. The bar wagon is by W H Lascelles & Co of the Finsbury Steam Joinery Works, a firm closely associated with the architect Norman Shaw who designed furniture for them from 1875 to 1885. The miniature clock tower on top of the wagon is almost identical to another

Lascelles contract, the Archway Tavern in North London. The British value their great craftsmen and engineers – Grinling Gibbons, Sheraton, Hepplewhite, Isambard Kingdom Brunel, Barnes Wallis, Alex Issigonis – just as highly as their artists: indeed in Adam, Chippendale, Capability Brown, William Morris, and Norman Shaw there is a considerable overlap. The Princess Louise is surely one of the country's greatest shrines of craftsmanship.

OPEN *all permitted hours*
STATION *Holborn tube*
BEERS *Sam Smith's range plus guests*
FOOD *meals & snacks lunchtime & evening*

THE SALISBURY
90 ST MARTIN'S LANE, WC2

Perhaps London's most famous late Victorian gin-palace, the Salisbury is as well-known for its theatreland location as its decor.

A tavern called the Coach & Horses stood on the site until 1866, when it was renamed the Salisbury Stores. The date and name together signify that the owner was taking advantage of Gladstone's 1860 Refreshment Houses Act. This sought to promote the sale of wine (which Gladstone thought wholesome and health-giving) against beer and spirits by lowering the duty on wine and permitting its sale without a licence. The 'Stores' element of the name commonly signified that liquor was available to take home as well as to drink on the premises: some pubs sold a third or a half of their stock as carry-outs.

In 1892 the old pub was pulled down and rebuilt as a restaurant. This was the time of the great pub-building boom, when many licensed houses were being suppressed, and those which survived were being lavishly and expensively redecorated.

The fantastic glasswork and art nouveaux bronze statuettes for which the Salisbury is famous date to its reopening as a pub in 1898, the climax of the boom and, as it turned out, the year before the bubble burst.

The profusely-decorated glasswork comprises mirrors and windows and acid-etched tableaux within brilliant-cut borders. Bronze nymphs serve the double purpose of dividing the separate seating areas and supporting small lamps, which grow out of the stalks of flowers they bear. The mahogany bar-back survives

intact, and the small private bar opening off St Martin's Court is a glory of ornate glass and wood. The pub is right in the middle of theatreland, and was a famed resort for actors and other show folk before the tourists drove them away. In fact, the pub itself had a brief celluloid career: it played the part of the Shaftesbury in the pioneering 1961 film *Victim*, starring Dirk Bogarde and dealing – daringly for the time – with the subject of homosexual blackmail. At about the same time its nickname

– it had been known as the Salisbury for years – became its official name.

OPEN *all permitted hours*
STATION *Leicester Sq tube*
BEERS *ScottishCourage range plus guests*
FOOD *meals & snacks 12-7.30*

Above The Salisbury's classic late-Victorian interior

The Sherlock Holmes
10 NORTHUMBERLAND ST, WC1

Until 1957 the Sherlock Holmes was the plain old Northumberland Arms, an unassuming and fairly typical Victorian pub noteworthy only as the last surviving building of its age and type in this heavily-redeveloped area. Built in 1846, the Northumberland Arms was one of literally hundreds of London pubs that underwent a substantial rebuilding in the 1890s – in the Northumberland's case 1891, when it was enlarged and given a new frontage.

At the same time a young Scottish writer, Arthur Conan Doyle, was just beginning to find fame and fortune with his fictional detective Sherlock Holmes: the first story, "A Study In Scarlet", had been published in 1887.

What brought Conan Doyle and this unexceptional neighbourhood boozer together? Well, just opposite the pub stood the Northumberland Hotel, a great gloomy edifice eventually pulled down to make way for the War Office. In its day, it was respectable enough to entertain country gentry visiting the Capital, and was chosen by Conan Doyle as a suitable location for the first meeting between the great detective and a Devonshire squire by the name of Sir Henry Baskerville.

Cut to the mid-1950s, and the aftermath of the Festival of Britain. One of the Festival exhibits, a tableau of Holmes's study at 221B Baker Street, had toured America and was now facing the scrapheap. But in 1957 someone at Whitbread had a brainstorm, bought the tableau, and installed it behind a glass screen in the upstairs room at the Northumberland Arms.

At the same time, the pub was renamed and its downstairs bar was decked out with more Holmes memorabilia (including a stuffed bloodhound's head, suitably daubed with fluorescent slobber, to represent the Hound of the Baskervilles) than you could shake a violin-bow at. Some call it Britain's first theme pub: I prefer to think of it as a tribute pub. The whole thing was a wild success, instantly overcoming the pub's rather unpromising location (it may be central and very handy, but it is somewhat tucked away and is actually invisible from the main tourist drag) and filling it with a babel of foreign tongues.

It helps that the pub is extraordinarily pretty, a real breath of fresh air in a corner of town which has been rendered utterly devoid of character by successive redevelopments.

OPEN *all permitted hours*
STATION *Charing Cross tube*
BEERS *Whitbread range*
FOOD *meals & snacks lunchtime & evening*
Restaurant

THE WEST END

The 'glittering' West End, mythical home of entertainment and celebrities, is where tourists flock by day to Oxford Street, the theatregoers by night to Drury Lane, and the hip and the chic mix coffee and cigarettes in the cafes and restaurants of Soho.

Soho was originally a hunting ground in the 17th century and takes its name from a hunting cry similar to 'Tally ho'. It has long been home to London's immigrant community – Italians, Greeks, Chinese and Poles – and is the traditional home of sleazy bohemia, haunted by hard drinking characters like Dylan Thomas and Francis Bacon. The peepshow glitz is now little more than window dressing and Soho is primarily home to London's gay scene and the media industry.

London is a city of contrasts and west of Regent's Street, Mayfair, traditionally the home of blue blooded aristocrats, and equally nowadays the home of multi-national corporations, is as grand an area as one is likely to find in the capital. However, some of its well-heeled residents may be surprised to know that it too had an underbelly of sleaze and sin in Victorian times when Shepherd's Market and its many pubs was a notorious centre for prostitution and crime.

Opposite The Shepherd's Tavern – once the haunt of prostitutes and low-life

THE ARGYLL ARMS
OXFORD CIRCUS, W1

Nothing about the Argyll's tall narrow exterior, dated 1868 and sandwiched between Oxford Circus tube and a rather drab office block – not even the most impressive display of ivy and pot-plants in London – prepares you for the brilliance of its interior.

The pub dates back to the 1740s, when the open fields to the North-west of London (the name Soho supposedly recalls the cry of the local hunt) were being developed, although there may have been a tavern on the site in the previous century.

The name comes from one of Marlborough's generals, whose London mansion was then where the Palladium now stands. But it's not the history of the Argyll that matters: it's the glass. Inside, three cosy private snugs lead off a long bar, separated by wood and glass partitions designed by Robert Sawyer in about 1895 and still miraculously intact. The riot of decoration, the trailing hop vines, the ornate plaster ceiling, the shining mahogany, have to be seen to be wondered at.

A long passage running behind them, divided from them by yet more of that wonderfully ornate glass, gives access to a much larger room and betrays the secret of the private snugs.

The Victorians are often accused of snobbery and a mania for privacy. It's an unfair charge. London in the 1880s and '90s was neither clean nor safe; and nor were a great many Londoners. A single big bar inevitably takes its tone from the drunkest, rowdiest element; and those who wished to avoid brawls or merely to converse at something below a hoarse scream need not be pilloried as class-bound bourgeois for seeking a little peace and quiet. The snugs gave them that, while more boisterous patrons could come and go along the rear passage without intruding.

That a pub of this magnificence should have survived the Luftwaffe and the brewery vandalism of the post-War years at all is a cause for celebration; that it should stand right beside one of the most important tube stations in tourists' London is surely proof of Divine providence.

OPEN *11-11 mon-sat, closed sun*
STATION *Oxford Circus tube*
BEERS *Carlsberg-Tetley range plus guests*
FOOD *meals & snacks lunchtime & evening*

THE AUDLEY

41 MOUNT ST, W1

The Audley is one of the most upmarket pubs in the West End. It is full of well-heeled tourists from America and Japan who bring high expectations along with their dollars and yen, and the highly professional staff are well capable of meeting their demands. And if the place feels more like the bar of a first-rate hotel than a pub, that's because the competition it has to beat is the Connaught, just around the corner. But it is a pub: a marvellous neo-French confection of red brick and pink terracotta, designed by the architect Thomas Verity and built by the brewer Watney's on the site of the Bricklayer's Arms, a pub of notoriously low repute, in 1889.

This was no act of philanthropy – even then, Watney's was not noted for philanthropy – but one of gamesmanship. At the time, London's magistrates were seeking to control the perceived problem of proliferating low beer-houses by refusing to renew licences – thus forcing the brewers to enlarge the pubs whose licences survived.

The shrinking noose that was thus put round the brewers' necks gave the Duke of Westminster's Grosvenor Estate, which owned the freehold here, a whip hand: it insisted that if Watney's wanted the lease renewed, it must pull down the Bricklayers altogether and replace it with something more respectable. This Watney's gladly did, building a grandiose pub that today finds itself in one of the most expensive shopping districts on the planet.

Yet despite the ornate exterior with its fantastically-carved stonework, the keynote inside is cool restraint. The mahogany and etched-glass partitions which once broke the pub into snugs are long gone, and the interior today is pleasantly airy and indeed almost austere in its restrained ornamentation. A distinctly superior place.

OPEN *all permitted hours*
STATION *Marble Arch tube*
BEERS *ScottishCourage range*
FOOD *meals & snacks*
lunchtime & evening
Garden

THE BARLEY MOW
DORSET ST, W1

I n the angle formed by Baker Street and Marylebone Road lies one of the least-known but most pleasant quarters of central London. The Portman Estate was mostly built in the late 18th century and is a quiet area where classy West End couturiers rub shoulders with old family ironmongers and the like for the complete convenience of the inhabitants of the spacious mansion flats above. It's affluent but understated – and in the Barley Mow it has a pub to match.

The Barley Mow is probably over 200 years old – in fact it was probably a country pub which got overlooked when the whole area was developed – but doesn't boast about it. The brass gin tap and price-lists are genuine and original, dating back to the early and mid 19th century, when take-home sales of gin were as significant as sales for consumption on the premises, and a spigot was far more convenient than a bottle.

But the Barley Mow's most distinctive features, the pine-panelled private booths along one side of the bar, are more recent: plain though they are, they belong to about 1890 when boxes of this sort enjoyed quite a vogue, and their construction has left isolated a third miniature bar, a tiny snug at the very back of the pub.

Legend has it that the pub doubled as the local pop-shop, and the landlord let these booths out to peripatetic pawnbrokers. A charming story, but given the respectable nature of the district, unlikely. The real genesis of the boxes lies in the Victorian mania for privacy, especially where liquor was concerned. Wealthy residential areas such as this normally included one or two pubs intended mainly for servants; but private boxes enabled master to sup alongside man without the embarrassment of being recognised.

Ironically, these tiny boxes were the high water-mark of the fashion in the 1880s and 90s for dividing and subdividing into ever more intimate spaces. From 1900 it became more common to open out small bars into large ones, and from the 1960s until the present day the fashion was for

great barn-like one-room bars. Now the tide is turning again, and booths are making their reappearance. These particular boxes are popular both with the Baker Street advertising men who make up the lunchtime trade

and the locals who use the Barley Mow in the evening: arrive early if you want to enjoy your ale and food in secluded splendour.

OPEN *mon-sat 11-11*
STATION *Baker St tube*
BEERS *Carlsberg-Tetley range plus guests*
FOOD *bar food 12-3.30*

THE FITZROY TAVERN
16 CHARLOTTE ST, W1

Not many London pubs have given their name to a whole district. Fitzrovia was merely an ill-defined and untitled quarter between Bloomsbury and Marylebone until someone decided that it needed a name, and that the best place to borrow a name from was its most prominent landmark, the Fitzroy Tavern.

The Tavern owes its name to the dalliances of Charles II: the Dukes of Grafton, who owned the land on which this part of London was built, were originally Royal by-blows and therefore surnamed Fitzroy.

That does not explain why this handsome but unexceptional red-brick pub, designed in 1897 by the prolific W M Brutton, should define the whole district. For that we have to look to its scandalous clientele from the 1920s to the 1950s, when under the long tenure of the Kleinfeld family, licensees from 1919 to 1956, the Fitzroy became a bastion of Bohemia.

This was largely a question of location: Soho and Bloomsbury were chock-a-block with artists and writers, and the Cleveland Street area was full of low-rent garrets in which a starving poet or painter might feel perfectly at home. In the 30s and early 40s Augustus John and Nina Hamnett (the Queen of Bohemia) held court here, and the party went on even during World war II and the blitz. In the 40s and 50s it was the proximity of Broadcasting House and the BBC that mattered: it was a mere five minutes' walk for such dedicated boozers as Dylan Thomas and Louis MacNiece and the set who surrounded them, as well as more sober broadcasters such as George Orwell. The pub now belongs to Sam Smith's and is not quite as Bohemian as it was, but there are plenty of photographs to remind one of the glory days.

OPEN *all permitted hours*
STATION *Goodge St tube*
BEERS *Sam Smith's range*
FOOD *meals & snacks lunchtime & evening*

THE FRENCH HOUSE
49 DEAN ST, W1

As a central but not especially grand quarter of London, Soho has long been a magnet for immigrants of entrepreneurial bent, and the French House is a living part of the district's cosmopolitan history. The York Minster, as it was known from the middle of the last century, was given the slang name the French Pub in the 1920s because it was run by a Belgian, Victor Berlemont, famed for his eccentric moustache. Francophone celebrities – including, naturellement, Maurice Chevalier – made a beeline for it, and in the war it became a natural rendezvous for French and Belgian officers including, they say, General de Gaulle himself.

Taken over after the war by son Victor's equally extravagantly moustached son Gaston, the French Pub changed its character somewhat and became a raffish hang-out for the hard-drinking Soho set of bohemians: Dylan Thomas left the script of *Under Milk Wood* on a stool. The aged but distinctly rakish habitués who congregate round one end of the bar on a quiet weekday doubtless remember the incident well.

Gaston Berlemont retired on Bastille Day 1989, and the pub was taken over by a couple of regulars too sensible to change anything (other than reopening the restaurant).

But even before the Berlemont dynasty began, the old York Minster represented multi-cultural Soho: a photograph of about 1910 shows it subtitled Schmitt's and advertising itself as a brandy shipper and purveyor of fine wines as well as a whisky blender and bar – it was, in fact, a licensed grocer catering to the quarter's immigrant populations, as well as a pub: The French House is from the outside an unassuming pub; and it's not much grander inside, either. But no-one has tried to force an identity on it: it is not a themed French pub. It is a pub which has a real character of its own, which happens to include 60 years of Belgian ownership. Oh, and in case there is any confusion, the French House is its official title, but it is still universally called the French Pub.

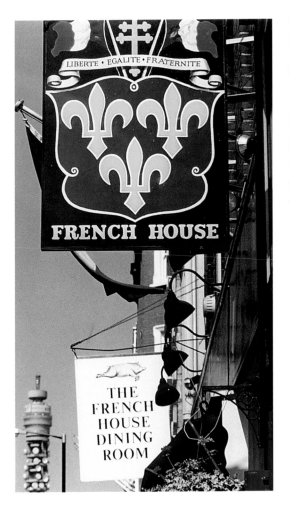

OPEN *12-11 mon-sat, 12-3, 7-10.30 sun*
STATION *Leicester Square tube*
BEERS *drink the wine*
FOOD *bar food lunchtime & evening Restaurant*

YE GRAPES

16 SHEPHERD'S MARKET, W1

As exuberant as its near-neighbour Shepherd's Tavern is dignified, the Grapes went up on the corner of Shepherd's Market in 1882. The market itself had long gone by then, and the area was given over to pleasure. The Cattle Bar at the Grapes was so named because livestock was traded there, but not the sort you find in country pastures.

The amount of prostitution in the Victorian era was astonishing, and was the perverse result of the very strictness of Victorian public morals. The Grapes could have been purpose-built for this commerce, and probably was. The most prominently-sited of the Shepherd's Market pubs, its brilliantly-lit exterior must have attracted those pleasure-seekers who strayed into the otherwise dimly-lit Market as a candle attracts moths.

Inside, as the number of fireplaces surviving attests, the pub was divided into those small intimate spaces which magistrates often tried to ban as conducive to vice. The polished woodwork, brilliant glass, and rich fabrics contributed to that ambience of foreign opulence. Today, the Grapes has a curiously mannish atmosphere – the product, largely, of the gun-room theme unifying the huge random collection of bric-à-brac that adorns the walls. Crossed skulls, matching flintlocks and a rather good long-case clock complement the myriad remnants, stuffed and mounted on plaques or in cases, of things that once walked, flew or swam.

An unconscious attempt to exorcise a racy past? Maybe. Certainly there's nothing remotely demi-monde about Grapes today. It is, though, an excellent free house with a fine range of ales and equally good food.

OPEN *all permitted hours*
STATION *Green Park tube*
BEERS *Whitbread range plus guests*
FOOD *meals & snacks lunchtime & evening*
Restaurant

THE GUINEA
30 BRUTON PLACE, W1

There has, apparently, been a pub on this site since 1423, although if you come in search of something genuinely medieval you will be disappointed, for all that you will find is a truly excellent mews pub of the late 18th century.

Curiously, the mews itself has been entirely replaced, by all appearances in the 1930s, except for the much older pub. This makes for a somewhat bizarre sight, but is not actually at all uncommon: pubs throughout London have survived the demolition of their neighbourhoods for the simple reason that they were making money. If you trawl East London, you will find windswept concrete slums of the 1950s and 60s well-larded with Victorian pubs still standing all alone, and still trading, where once were busy street-corners.

Whether or not there was a tavern here in the reign of Henry VI, there was certainly one in the reign of Charles II, when the aristocratic Berkeley family of Bruton in Somerton started developing their Middlesex estate.

Originally the pub was known as the Pound after the cattle and hog pound which then existed where Berkeley Square now stands. Its name changed as a joke in 1663 when the first golden guinea, then worth a pound, was struck. All right, not a very sophisticated joke; but these are farm boys we are dealing with.

It changed its name again in 1717, unofficially this time, when the guinea was revalued at £1-1s, to the One Pound One. Again, not a good joke, but one that has stood the test of time, since it is now known almost as well by this nickname as by its proper one.

So it continued for many generations as an unspectacular but prosperous mews pub providing for the servants of the great – the very great, given its location – seeing nothing more spectacular

than a makeover in the 19th century, from which today's decorative scheme of plain timber and nicotine-coloured plaster comes, until the 1950s, when someone developed a truly great restaurant in the back snug.

Frank Sinatra, Richard Burton and Elizabeth Taylor, Princess Margaret and King Hussein are among the mixed bag of celebrities who have come here for the very best of English fare, including steak and kidney pies (puddings, really, since their crusts contain an enlivening handful of suet) which win prize after prize after prize.

You don't have to be a celebrity to eat here, though. The Guinea is a very friendly and unpretentious place, where slightly pixillated regulars are just as welcome as Eastern Mediterranean royalty.

OPEN *11-11 mon-fri, 11-3, 7-11 sat, closed sun*
STATION *Green Park tube*
BEERS *Young's range*
FOOD *meals lunchtime & evening snacks lunchtime*
Restaurant

THE OLD COFFEE HOUSE

49 BEAK ST, W1

Talk of coffee-houses brings to mind the establishments of the late 17th and early 18th centuries, where politicians and businessmen gathered to drink the fashionable and expensive new beverage, to meet clients, to confer, to conspire – to network, in fact. Today's Tory party was founded in a coffee-house, as was Lloyd's of London.

However, it is not these early establishments which give this particular pub its heritage; for there were two subsequent generations of coffee-house.

The first appeared in the 1820s and 30s in response to the challenge of the gin-palaces and beerhouses, which were beginning to multiply at the time and which sold no food.

These coffee-houses did, providing like the greasy spoons of today an affordable and alcohol-free eating-house, where working men could victual themselves without temptation. They also offered a free read of the newspapers for the serious and dedicated men who founded the Trade Unions, Friendly Societies and Co-operatives through which the Victorian working class advanced itself. Coffee-houses appeared again in 1867 as the temperance movement's attempt to carry the war to the enemy by providing establishments which imitated the pub in every detail but one: they sold no alcohol. Even then they sold alcohol substitutes: Anti-Burton, Winterine and the like.

High-minded aristocrats and non-conformist businessmen alike queued up to plough fortunes into these worthy ventures. Unfortunately, and unlike the previous generation of coffee-house owners, they could not resist preaching. The tendency in them to try to improve people was

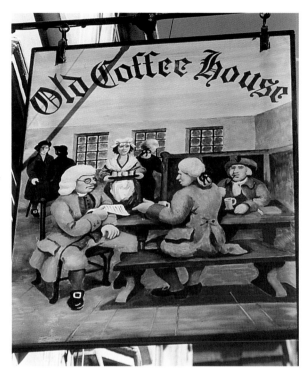

too strong, and as people hate being preached at, they stayed away in droves. Ironically, these mock-pubs made perfect real pubs, and many of them, including this one, ended up serving the very opposite of their original intention. Today, the Old Coffee House is a large, cluttered, one-bar Soho local, full of cheery bric-à-brac and equally cheery businessmen.

OPEN *all permitted hours*
STATION *Oxford Circus tube*
BEERS *ScottishCourage range*
FOOD *meals lunchtime*

THE SHEPHERD'S TAVERN
50 HERTFORD ST, SHEPHERD MARKET, W1

Mayfair has long been one of the most expensive and exclusive residential areas in the Western World, but it didn't start out that way. Originally known as Brookfield, the area was renamed when the May hiring fair – an annual event at which servants found employers, and subsequently a more general market – was moved from the Haymarket in 1688. It was evidently a rowdy affair, proving a magnet for prostitutes, as well as colourful street-traders such as Tiddy Dol, the dandified gingerbread seller whose name was taken for the vast restaurant opposite Shepherd's Tavern.

In the 1720s and 30s the area was laid out and redeveloped by an architect named Edward Shepherd, who is also said to have designed the pub that bears his name as well as a now-vanished market-hall which boasted a shambles below and an assembly room (surely a very smelly one) above. Still the low-life reputation clung, and Shepherd Market remained notorious for prostitution well into modern times.

It may come as a surprise that such a well-known red-light enclave was permitted in so well-heeled an area. But London, unlike Paris, had few brothels, and since the authorities saw prostitution as a problem of containment rather than suppression, every affluent area had its street or, in this case, knot of streets, where blind eyes were turned provided certain niceties were observed.

Of course, things have changed since then: it has been said that Shepherd Market used to be full of affluent men furtively enjoying better sex than they could get at home, whereas today it is full of affluent men furtively enjoying better lunches than they can get at home.

Shepherd's Tavern seems too dignified ever to have been a pick-up joint, however discreet. Its well-proportioned ground-floor bar, with elegant bow window, fine carved mahogany bar-fitting and elegant

staircase, has a Georgian mien quite unlike the naughty nineties exuberance of its near-neighbour the Grapes.

OPEN *all permitted hours*
STATION *Green Park tube*
BEERS *ScottishCourage range*
FOOD *meals & snacks lunchtime & evening*

WESTMINSTER CHELSEA & KENSINGTON

Westminster is where the power is. Kensington is where those
who wield the power live. Chelsea is where those power-wielding
residents spend their leisure time. This simplified view gives at
least some coherence to this part of our tour.

W estminster is home of the Abbey, the Houses of Parliament
and the civil service warrens they call Whitehall. The pubs are steeped in
the history of power-broking, they have witnessed the execution of kings
and are still the place where MPs imbibe between votes.

The Royal Borough of Kensington and Chelsea is one of the most
beautiful cityscapes on the planet and the home of big shopping –
Harrods, Harvey Nichols and the King's Road. The elegant, imposing
mansion-blocks that tower over the plane-trees are the nearest England
comes to the gracious apartment-blocks of the great cities of the
Continent. Many of the pubs in these parts were built to serve the senior
servants of the great Georgian houses. The whole area has a terrific magic
for out-of-towners and is a wonderful place to wander aimlessly between
purchases and pubs.

Above Duke of York Street in SW1, home to the Red Lion

THE ADMIRAL CODRINGTON
17 MOSSOP ST, SW3

The Admiral Cod has this much in common with the Anglesea Arms (qv) half a mile away: it's in what used to be a market-gardening area, and it's named after a hero of the Napoleonic War. The first we know because what is now Mossop Street was, in the early part of the last century, Green Lettuce Lane, and is marked on a map of 1822 as running into fields roughly between Draycott Avenue and Sloane Street. Why it was renamed Mossop Street is a matter for your own conjecture.

As for Admiral Sir Edward Codrington, he was already a naval officer of great experience when he commanded the Orion at Trafalgar, accepting the surrender of the French ship the Intrepide and her captain, with whom he became great friends and who spent his period as a prisoner of war as a guest in Codrington's house.

Codrington went on to command the combined English, Russian and French fleets at Navarino Bay in 1827, when the combined Turkish and Egyptian fleets were beaten and as a result of which Greece gained its independence – the cause in which the romantic poet Lord Byron had lost his life three years earlier. The admiral died in 1855, covered in glory.

The old market-gardening district was thoroughly developed by 1860; but today's Admiral Codrington dates from about 1900 and although its surroundings do it no favours – the John Lewis warehouse occupies the whole of the other side of Mossop Street, and the former Harrod's Warehouse looms large on Draycott Avenue – it has a pleasant, almost rustic atmosphere.

The older part is divided into three very traditional bars decked out in dark matchboard dadoes and decorated with a few well-chosen prints. It has bowed sash windows, bare floorboards, and a pleasant little garden to one side. The covered-over rear courtyard, by contrast, has a kind of cool Tuscan chic, with its marble tiled floor, glass roof, and pale timber furniture.

In the early 1980s the Admiral Cod was one of the headquarters of Sloanedom: among the regulars, so they say, was a bashful young kindergarten teacher, one Lady Diana Spencer.

OPEN *all permitted hours*
STATION *South Kensington tube*
BEERS *Bass ales*
FOOD *meals lunchtime & evening, snacks lunchtime*
Garden

THE ALBERT

52 VICTORIA ST, SW1

In the modern glass canyon of Victoria Street, the Albert is an isolated and welcome survivor. First recorded in 1831 as the Blue Coat Boy after the famous charity school nearby, it was rebuilt by architect J Carter Woods in 1862 to be the tap for the Artillery Brewery, one of a number of breweries in what was then a busy district of industry and enterprise, rather than the Government ghetto it is today. At the same time it was renamed in honour of the great Prince Consort, who had died of typhoid the year before.

One of these local breweries was Watney's, whose Stag Brewery was no more than 200 yards away – in Stag Place, unsurprisingly. In 1898 Watney's merged with two other London brewers, Combe's and Reid's, expressly to cash in on the current pub-buying and pub-building boom. The new company immediately floated on the Stock Market, and the Albert was one of its first purchases.

The Albert has had all of its inner partitions removed but retains many original features and has the atmosphere of solid respectability appropriate to a clientele which includes senior civil servants and MPs. There is a division bell in the dining room upstairs, and signed photographs of Prime Ministers past and present line the stairs.

OPEN *all permitted hours*
STATION *St James's Park & Victoria tubes*
BEERS *ScottishCourage range plus guests*
FOOD *Meals & snacks lunchtime & evening*
Wheelchair access

ANGLESEA ARMS
215 SELWOOD TERRACE, SW7

The affluent and fashionable residential quarter that lies between Chelsea and South Kensington was, 200 years ago, one of the areas of market gardens which surrounded the capital. The name of the district then, Queen's Elm, survives today as a single small square just south of Fulham Road; and the name of one of the little landowners who grew lettuces for London in the 18th century survives bizarrely in the name of the western side of this pleasant street.

Presumably when Salad Lane, as the street then was, came to be built up in about 1830, Mr Selwood was only thought important enough to have half of it named after him: the other side is called Neville Terrace; and if there is another instance in London of a street having one name on one side and another on the other, I don't know of it.

The Anglesea Arms is on Mr Selwood's side of the street, and is named after Henry William Paget, Marquess of Anglesey, the English cavalry commander at Waterloo responsible, with Wellington, for one of the most laconic exchanges ever recorded in warfare.

Having just been struck a glancing blow by a cannon-ball, Paget looked down, turned to Wellington, and remarked: "By God, Sir, I think I've lost my leg." To which Wellington replied: "By God, Sir, I think you have." Paget had the leg pickled, and it was buried with him when he died in 1854.

The Anglesea Arms was new when Charles Dickens knew it in 1835; he lodged at number 11 while

courting Catherine Hogarth, who lived nearby. After they were married, he took her on his American tour of 1842.

Everywhere the Dickenses went they were greeted rapturously and fêted bibulously; and when the American temperance campaigners satirised Dickens for his drinking it is notable that they included Catherine in their comments. Their table was notoriously liquid – had that anything to do with his constant criticisms of her forgetfulness and her lack of self-esteem, I wonder? At any rate, they separated amid a lengthy, messy, and very public scandal in 1858.

Dickens would not know the smart but comfortable Anglesea Arms of today. The whole has been knocked into one big, airy bar, with the exception of a cosy little snug known as the cubby which has a rather nice little cast iron and tilework fireplace. One end of the main bar is all leather sofas, like the fellows' common room of some ancient college; the other end is more traditionally kitted out with pews and partitions. Blissfully, there is no jukebox, fruit machine or television, lending the pub a welcome traditional atmosphere.

The pub achieved fame among beer-lovers in the 1970s as a free house which provided vital patronage for small independent ale brewers.

OPEN *11-11 mon-fri, 11-4, 7-11 sat, 12-4, 7-10.30 sun*
STATION *South Kensington tube*
BEERS *free house*
FOOD *meals & snacks lunchtime*

THE ANTELOPE
22 EATON TERRACE, SW1

You'll find this hard to believe, but the opulent streets and squares you strolled through on your way to the Antelope were once one of the most desolate, dangerous, and noxious parts of London. Known as the Five Fields, the whole stretch of land from the back of Buckingham Palace Gardens, between what are now Sloane Street and Grosvenor Place, and stretching almost down the Thames was a dreary swamp through which the polluted Westbourne carried its cargo of sewage and refuse. Edgar Allan Poe knew it as a schoolboy, and in 1817 described it as a place where:

> A barren waste existed, fetid, damp,
> Cheered by the ray of no enlivening lamp.
> A marshy spot where not a patch of green,
> No stunted scrub nor sickly flower was seen,
> But all things base, the refuse of the town,
> Loathsome and rank, in one foul mess are thrown.

Only 100 yards from where the Antelope now stands was the notorious Bloody Bridge, which carried the King's Road over the River Westbourne and which derived its name from the local bandits' preference for silencing their victims for good.

The great builder Thomas Cubitt changed all that in 1827 when he diverted and channelled the Westbourne and drained the swamp, using the clay which had previously prevented it from draining itself to make bricks, and importing thousands of tonnes of porous gravel on which Belgravia, yet another corner of the Duke of Westminster's vast London estate, could be built.

Accounts of the Antelope's antecedents vary: some say it was an isolated (and if so, surely villainous) country pub at least 50 years before Cubitt arrived; others that it was purpose-built, like the Nag's Head and

Star Tavern, for the servants of the grand houses of the area. Whether built for them or not, they were its principal custom once the houses had gone up, along with the small tradesman whose businesses depended on the custom of the rich – and on the favour of the senior servants who actually did the shopping.

Today's Antelope would not seem alien to the ghost of a Victorian housekeeper: it retains its sober, modest, decorative scheme of island bar, etched glass, wooden high-backed settles, bareboard floor, planked ceiling and panelled dado – for it would not have done to be too flashily ornate.

The principal changes have been the addition of a restaurant in what would have been a private parlour upstairs and the loss certainly of one partition, possibly of two, in the main area. But the separate snug where the grander butlers would have reigned in splendour is still intact.

OPEN *all permitted hours*
STATION *Sloane Square tube*
BEERS *Carlsberg-Tetley range plus guests*
FOOD *meals & snacks lunchtime*
Restaurant

Above The Antelope – a Victorian butler's retreat

BUNCH OF GRAPES
207 BROMPTON RD, SW3

The "local" for Harrod's, not to mention the Brompton Oratory and the museums of South Kensington, is a suitably precious little gem, with some of the best glass in London. The pub goes back to the days before the architect Henry Holland started the development of the area in the 1780s and 90s by widening and straightening the lane connecting Old Brompton with Knightsbridge and lining it with upper middle-class housing. This project he dubbed "Hans Town", a name which never stuck but is remembered in the title of the Act of Parliament by which he proceeded.

However, the development of Hans Town was modest compared to what followed; a map of 1822 shows Brompton Road surrounded by fields on both sides: according to the historian Percy Fitzgerald, writing in the 1890s, these were mainly market gardens and included a fairground.

By the middle of the 19th century, the entire area was built over and had achieved much the shape we see today. And as the villas and mansion-blocks rose, so the old Bunch of Grapes – first recorded in 1770 – metamorphosed to keep up with the expectations of its customers.

The pub's external form dates to a

rebuilding of 1844, when the villages of Knightsbridge, Brompton, and Old Brompton disappeared under the ashlar Alps that define the district today. But the perfect interior for which the pub is famous is more recent still: the lobby mirror is signed by William James & Co of Camden Town (whose later works included the dazzling Assembly Rooms in Kentish Town) and dated 1875.

The two tiled lobbies with their painted mirrors, mahogany arches, and brown granite columns lead into three comfortable bars, one of them marked out by a window engraving as the former "bottle & glass" sales area, all divided by etched glass and carved mahogany screens. The pub has just been refurbished but its two greatest treasures – a hand-carved house sign representing a bunch of grapes and, for some reason, bullrushes; and a working set of snob screens also etched with bunches of grapes – have been zealously preserved.

The old functions room upstairs is now a restaurant.

OPEN *all permitted hours*
STATION *South Kensington tube*
BEERS *ScottishCourage range*
FOOD *meals & snacks lunchtime & evening*
Restaurant

THE NAG'S HEAD
53 KINNERTON ST, SW1

The Nag's Head almost certainly started life as the early 19th-century equivalent of a car rental business: the name was often used by publicans with a sideline in livery, or renting out horses; and the bar is so tiny that generations of landlords must surely have had some other source of income.

Kinnerton Street was built in the 1820s as a mews to serve the great houses of Wilton Place, which was part of the enormous Grosvenor Estate. It's a humble street of little artisans' cottages and servants' pubs, and nothing much changed in its first 150 years.

The same was true of the Nag's Head: in the century to 1960, it had had only five landlords and was always reckoned to be London's smallest pub. In the early 1970s the semi-basement at the back was opened up as a second bar, robbing it of its claim but not of its charm.

However, somewhere it lost its way: in the 70s it suffered several changes of licensee and eventually closed down altogether. It was boarded up for several months before the present landlords, ex-stuntman

Kevin Moran and his actor son Peter, arrived in 1979 to breathe the life back into it.

The Nag's Head is most definitely a bric-à-brac pub. It had the foundations when the Morans arrived: a curiously low bar-counter; a mid-19th century beer engine with little Chelsea china beer-pulls; a fine big fireplace with cast-iron range; wood-panelled walls; brown lincrusta ceiling; and what looks suspiciously like genuine lino on the floor.

To this has been added a collection of odds and ends so bizarre, so eclectic, so haphazard as to shame the paltry assortments of tawdry tat that modern pub designers buy in bulk from the repro warehouse and try to pass off as bric-à-brac.

The prizes of the collection are two 1930s penny-in-the-slot amusement machines, one of them a one-armed bandit, the other a variant on the "what-the-butler-saw" theme: old pennies are kept behind the bar, and all profits go to charity.

OPEN *all permitted hours*
STATION *Knightsbridge tube*
BEERS *Carlsberg-Tetley beers plus guests, especially Adnams*
FOOD *meals & snacks lunchtime & evening*

Above The Nag's Head – a tiny box of bric-à-brac curios

PHENE ARMS
9 PHENE ST, SW3

This cosy backstreet pub in Chelsea is not one you'll find in many guidebooks – yet. But if the refurbishers can keep their itchy fingers off it, it will, in a few years' time, become a much-visited collector's piece, I promise it.

The pub itself was built in 1851-3 by the wealthy landowner Dr John Samuel Phene (pronounced Feeney), who lived in a house nearby packed with architectural curios and also built one or two of the neighbouring streets.

Phene's reputation stems from his great innovation as an improver of town planning: tree-lined streets. It seems blindingly obvious now as the simplest possible way of improving the townscape, but nobody had thought of it before; and if you're that sort of person you can almost date London streets by whether they have trees. No trees, pre-Phene; trees, post-Phene.

Like all prototypes, there were glitches: Dr Phene favoured acacias, which tend to be too twisty and bushy to be ideal (some of them, or their descendants, survive

in the pub's rather pleasant garden); elms, limes, poplars and planes soon took over. Nevertheless, the idea found favour in very high places: Prince Albert and Queen Victoria loved it, and interpolated it into the plans for the South Kensington museum district. When it was also adopted by Baron Hausmann, the great rebuilder of Paris, its future was assured.

But that's not what the Phene Arms is really all about: what it's really all about is retro-chic. The new Watney Combe Reid combine bought it just before the (by then) unbelievably ancient Dr Phene died in 1912, and sometime around 1960 that brewery's inimitable interior designers chose it as a subject for their particular and peculiar brand of magic.

The crow-stepped tiled fireplace. The brass lamps with their red shades. The artificially-grained plywood-fronted bar, with its barleysugar-twist wrought-iron spindles supporting a minimalist plywood gantry. The plush. The carpets. The place is a shrine to the belief which flourished from about 1958 to 1968 that pubs in places like Chelsea ought to mimic the cocktail bars of West End hotels. One half expects to find Roger Moore as The Saint buying Diana Rigg as Emma Peel a maraschino cobbler with Ian Hendry, Bryan Forbes and Laurence Harvey nursing martinis (with olives, of course) in the oh-so-sophisticated background.

It's easy to be sarcastic about this kind of decor now, but in 10 years' time it will be unique. It will probably be listed by the Heritage Department. Basket meals, fondues, and things flambeed at your table will be compulsory in the upstairs restaurant. It will probably even spearhead a Watney's Red Barrel revival. I'll be there, if only I can find my good old Chelsea boots.

OPEN *all permitted hours*
STATION *Sloane Square tube*
BEERS *ScottishCourage range*
FOOD *meals & snacks lunchtime & evening*
Garden
Restaurant

RED LION
23 CROWN PASSAGE, SW1

One of the joys of London is discovering a half-hidden passageway where, amid the grandest commercial streets in the world, you suddenly stumble into a secret world of small, quiet, unassuming shops and pubs known only to the few habitués who haunt the place.

Crown Passage is just such an alley, running between two of Mayfair's busiest thoroughfares, King Street and Pall Mall, yet almost invisible to most of those who hurry past. The more leisurely explorer, however, will find first an old-fashioned cobbler, then an ironmonger's, and finally an ancient London pub, the Red Lion. This small half-timbered pub claims to be London's second-oldest continuously licensed house, although giving no hint of which might be the oldest. If the claim is true, the Red Lion is at least 350 years old, and may well be older, since this part of Mayfair, St James's, was first developed in Tudor times.

Once past the hanging baskets and leaded lights, the L-shaped panelled bar shows no obvious sign of great age; the reverse, in fact: it is timeless, and could easily have inspired Trollope in his description of the Cat & Whistle:

"It was one of those small tranquil shrines of Bacchus in which the god is worshipped perhaps with as constant devotion, though with less noisy demonstrations of zeal, than in his larger and more public temples. None absolutely of the lower orders were encouraged to come thither for oblivion. It had about it nothing inviting to the general eye. No gas illuminations proclaimed its midnight grandeur. No reiterated assertions in gaudy letters a foot long as to the merits of the old tom seduced the thirsty traveller."

Old pubs like this attract charming but unlikely stories. In the Red Lion's case, the tale is that Nell Gwynne used to live in Pall Mall, and used a secret tunnel connecting the pub's cellars with those of St James's Palace to pay clandestine visits to her lover, Charles II.

Apart from the fact that discretion never seemed to trouble Charles II, who openly acknowledged and usually ennobled his mistresses and bastards, the Red Lion does not actually lie between Pall Mall and the palace. A supposed access point is more likely to be part of the pub's foundations, or possibly the entrance to a 17th-century cess-pit.

Still, it's a nice story.

OPEN *11-11 mon-fri, 11-4 sat. Closed sun*
TUBE *Green Park tube*
BEERS *ScottishCourage beers plus guests*
FOOD *meals & snacks lunchtime Restaurant upstairs.*

RED LION
2 DUKE OF YORK ST, SW1

L ike the Argyll Arms at Oxford Circus, the Red Lion is all about glass. A small pub, clearly meant to satisfy the needs of the servants and tradespeople associated with the surrounding mansions, the Red Lion was built in the 1820s and given its present frontage – which is neat but frankly unremarkable – by an otherwise-unknown architect called Rawlings in 1871.

What lifts it out of the ordinary is its amazing array of brilliant-cut and acid-etched mirrors, all flowers and writhing tendrils, held in elegantly-arched mahogany frames. The glass appears to date from about

Above The Red Lion in Crown Passage

1890, the great period of plate-glass technology, and was probably the work of Walter Gibbs & Sons of Blackfriars.

The question that will doubtless rise to your lips, when you have overcome your wonder at the brilliance of the display, is: why? Why should anyone go to such trouble and expense to deck out such a humble neighbourhood bar to such an extravagant degree? The answers are two: speculation and prostitution. In the first place, many such decorative schemes were installed by landlords who intended to sell up, taking advantage of the fierce competition for good sites raging between London brewers and interlopers from Burton. A modern and lavish interior was a sure way of driving up the bidding; in the case of the Red Lion, the Burton interloper Ind Coope bid highest.

In the second place, casual prostitution was endemic among the scandalously underpaid women workers of the time, and the myriad small parlours and snugs of contemporary pubs were feared by the magistrates to be the scenes of many a tryst. Mirrors were the answer favoured by magistrates, to allow the landlord overall supervision of the whole interior from a single vantage-point. Indeed in some licensing divisions, frosting of the external windows was not permitted above five feet from the ground, so that passing constables could peer in and ensure that public morals were not being outraged.

Of course, the mirrors can also be taken at their aesthetic face-value: glittering and sparkling gems that made the Red Lion – and still make it – a beautiful place to sup.

OPEN *11-11 mon-sat*
STATION *Piccadilly Circus tube*
BEERS *Carlsberg-Tetley range plus guests*
FOOD *meals & snacks lunchtime*

Above The Red Lion in Duke of York Street

RED LION
48 PARLIAMENT ST, SW1

There have been pubs on this site since at least 1434, under a variety of names – it has been the Hopping Hall and the Rose as well as the Red Lion – and ownerships: it was Crown property for a good few centuries and then belonged to the now defunct Cannon Brewery.

The present Red Lion – or at any rate, the carcass of it, for it has been much altered since – dates to 1733. In 1824 it was the scene of a seemingly trivial incident in the childhood of Charles Dickens, then 12 and fending for himself by working in a shoe-black factory while his parents were in debtor's prison. Evidently, though, it made a deep impression on him, for he resurrected it for use in David Copperfield.

"'What is your best, your VERY best, ale a glass?' 'Twopence halfpenny,' says the landlord, 'is the price of the Genuine stunning ale.' 'Then,' says I, producing the money, 'just draw me a glass of the Genuine Stunning, if you please, with a good head to it.'"

Alas for David! – for his brave attempt to appear grown-up and

manly was met with intolerable condescension; he was given his money back, along with a motherly pat, by the landlady; and by the landlord a glass of ale which was neither Genuine (home-brewed) nor Stunning (extra-strong)."

The original Red Lion was entirely remodelled by the rather superior architects Shoebridge & Rising in 1896 to suit a very superior clientele: the pub is one of a number in the environs of Parliament to have a division bell to summon MPs back to the House for a vote. It is also the nearest pub to 10 Downing Street; but although almost all PMs ritually profess a fondness for traditional British ale, none of them seems to pop into their local. Much of the work of 1896 survives, although as is almost always the case the original partitions have been removed. But there is still a fine mahogany bar-fitting, some good glass, and a magnificent coffered plaster ceiling to be seen.

OPEN *all permitted hours*
STATION *Westminster tube*
BEERS *Carlsberg-Tetley beers*
FOOD *meals & snacks lunchtime*
Restaurant

THE SILVER CROSS
33 WHITEHALL, SW1

At the Trafalgar Square end of Whitehall, on the left as you go down, is a group of three pubs; and although the Old Shades and the Clarence are the best-known and most written-about, actually it's the Silver Cross – the Cinderella of the three, although it would be defamatory to call the other two Ugly Sisters – which is the most interesting.

The site was recorded as a hermitage in 1235 and 1370; although since Whitehall was a political hub even then, it can hardly have been the sort of isolated "desert" that hermits supposedly sought. Perhaps the inhabitant was a lobbyist for hermits everywhere. Or, more likely, it was a house of Cistercians, who described themselves as hermits even though they lived communally.

Today's Silver Cross, however, belongs to the 17th rather than the 14th century. In the early 17th century it was the London home of a very important individual indeed: Sir William Waad MP, clerk to the Privy Council, Lieutenant of the Tower of London, and an investigator of Jesuitical plotters in the fevered anti-Catholic London of the time.

In the middle of the century, the house was bought by one Joseph Craig, who in 1674 converted it into an inn. Now inns in

this most royal part of town are licensed not by the local justices, as are pubs in more humdrum parts, but by the Board of Green Cloth, which is an office of Buckingham Palace. (To this day the licensee has to make that intimidating trip to the Palace every year to get his renewal – although it's a functionary, not Herself, who chairs the hearing.)

It happens that Joseph Craig was a member of the Board of Green Cloth, so he could more or less guarantee that his premises would continue to trade unmolested. No wonder the Craig family owned it for 135 years: it must have paid generations of school fees.

At any rate, the pub's character is still rooted in the 17th century, and although what you see may be replacements or reproductions, the panelling, the small fireplace with its oak overmantel, and the massive wagon-vaulting with its vine motif are sufficiently period in feel to make one spare a thought for Charles I, stepping out through the Banqueting Hall window to his death that chilly January morning in 1649.

OPEN *all permitted hours*
STATION *Charing Cross tube*
BEERS *ScottishCourage range*
FOOD *meals & snacks lunchtime & evening*

Above A vine motif decorates the Silver Cross near Trafalgar Square

THE STAR TAVERN
6 BELGRAVE MEWS WEST, SW1

Like the Nag's Head and the Antelope, the Star Tavern is a late Georgian mews pub intended to serve the servants of the great houses being built on the Grosvenor Estate. But there the similarities end, for the Star, tucked away though it is, is a very much grander affair and is proof of the social divisions that once existed even within the ranks of domestic servants, who derived their status from the status of their employers and guarded it just as jealously.

The ground floor of the pub was originally divided into at least three rooms. The main entrance opens on to a public bar which may at one time have been subdivided by partitions around the horseshoe bar-counter. Here one can imagine grooms and footmen assembling on their rare days off. Off to the left was an elegant saloon with its own fireplace, where valets and butlers might foregather.

But penetrate this room, and at the back of the pub you would have found yourself in the true inner sanctum where only the butlers of the

very grandest houses – and the grandest houses in this part of London were, at the height of Empire, the grandest houses in the world – would have congregated, snubbing any lesser mortals who presumed to enter.

Domestic service was, before the First World War, the single largest employer in the country, and represented one of the few chances of social advancement for working-class people. In the status-obsessed Victorian world the difference between the harrassed skivvy of a small shopkeeper and the butler of one of the great houses of Belgrave Square was a gulf as great as that which divided their respective employers.

All the different rooms and bars were knocked into two at some point after the Second World War, and the rigid social categorisation of earlier days went with them. At the time, the Star Tavern was run by one of those "characters" who surface from time to time in the pub world; and Paddy Kennedy was very much of his time.

Resolutely uncowed by the status of his patrons, Paddy became legendary for refusing point-black to serve anyone he didn't like the look of. The people he did like the look of were the demi-monde of gangsters and foreign aristos who haunted the West End in those days: Billy Hill rubbed shoulders with the Gaekwar of Baroda; the Great Train Robbers did a bit of informal plotting in what was then a private room upstairs; and if Christine Keeler and Mandy Rice-Davies didn't stop off for a few liveners on their way to a night on the tiles, they jolly well should have.

OPEN *11.30-3 mon-thurs, 11.30-11 fri, 11.30-3,
6.30-11 sat, 12-3 7-10.30 sun*
STATION *Hyde Park Corner tube*
BEERS *Fuller's range*
FOOD *meals & snacks lunchtime & evening weekdays only*

WEST LONDON

From a distance West London gives the false impression of being
a sea of slate roofs. This view from the elevated sections of the
Westway as you enter London is about as uninspiring as views of
the capital get. You have to get down off the Westway to find
out just how misleading this impression is.

West London is packed with characterful districts from the
multi-cultural Latin Quarter feel of Notting Hill where eerily calm
Sunday mornings are the perfect cure to frenetic Saturday nights, to the
well-heeled tranquillity of Little Venice with its houseboats and villas.
You just have to be close to the ground to get the vibe.

Like much of London, the area was developed from farmland
throughout the 19th century to accommodate the fast-growing
population. It developed its share of pubs offering the usual fantasies:
countrified yeoman idylls like the Archery Tavern and Windsor Castle,
alongside the racy gin-palace pomp of the Warrington. This section also
includes a couple of true country gems from as far west as Uxbridge and
Hampton Court.

Opposite The Prince Alfred – poetry in glass & mahogany

THE ARCHERY TAVERN
4 BATHURST RD, W2

That such a quiet sidestreet, and such a quiet pub, can exist within yards of the roaring traffic of the Bayswater Road is one of the little surprises that gives London its charm. The area was developed in 1839-40 as London continued its outward spread, and as often happened with speculative building, this unassuming, almost countrified pub was the first building to go up. It was probably completed and open for business before ground was even broken on the great squares and terraces of prosperous Bayswater; the reason being that it provided the builder with at least some cash-flow, and if things went wrong, he had a going concern to sell to offset his losses.

The proximity of Hyde Park – scarcely 100 yards away, but thanks to the traffic not so easy to get to nowadays – guaranteed that the pub, originally called the Crown, should not long remain the haunt of shopkeepers and servants. Hyde Park was one of the few places where the well-to-do of mid-Victorian London could get a breath of fresh air and a spot of exercise, with riding in Rotten Row and archery on butts at Lancaster Gate used by the Royal Toxophilite Society.

Archery went through something of a vogue among the genteel classes of the time, partly because it was one of the few sports (along with croquet) sedate enough for corseted and

crinolined gentlewomen to enjoy.

The change of name was a clear attempt to attract the users of the butts; and although the Toxophilites (lovers of the bow) eventually moved west to Kensington Gardens, the connection is recalled both in the inn-sign and the 19th-century prints that decorate the bars.

As for the pub itself, it is a real haven amid the fumes. The original layout of three small bars and a fourth which is not much more than a corridor, all grouped around a central island bar, survives intact. The decor is rustic, with a plain dado of pine panels giving the feel of the servants' hall of some old-fashioned manor-house; the high-backed settles in the little room at the back would belong in any old country inn; and the only concession to London is the ornate moulding of cornice and ceiling.

The country atmosphere is enhanced by the range of ales: the Archery Tavern is one of the few outlets in the capital for Hall & Woodhouse beers from Dorset.

OPEN *all permitted hours*
STATION *Lancaster Gate tube*
Beers *Hall & Woodhouse beers*
FOOD *meals lunchtime & evening*
Garden

CROWN & TREATY
90 OXFORD RD, UXBRIDGE

RURAL Middlesex largely vanished beneath the suburban development that followed the extension of the Underground in the 1920s and '30s, and there is little evidence left of a more bucolic past. But amid the shopping precincts, housing estates and factories, there are odd reminders of what the county must once have looked like.

One such is the Crown & Treaty which, with its small bricks and big chimneys, was built as a substantial home for a well-off local family in 1576. The original stone fireplace, a model of Elizabethan opulence, survives in the bar. In those days the house had an extra wing and a large garden running down to the River Colne, but they were sacrificed when the coach road to Oxford went through in 1785.

The house came by its name thanks to the events of 1645, the climax of the English Civil War, when it was the scene of peace talks between Royalists and Parliament. The talks lasted for 20 days but came to nothing, for both sides thought they were winning. Although the King's northern armies under Prince Rupert had just been annihilated by Cromwell at Marston Moor, Charles had won what he thought was an equally decisive victory over the Earl of Essex at Lostwithiel in Cornwall. Events were to prove Charles wrong within a year; but for the time being neither side was disposed to compromise, and the talks collapsed.

The room where the talks were held, called the Treaty Room even though nothing was signed, is still to be seen with its original dark oak panelling and some contemporary furniture. The panelling has its own story: it was dismantled and sold in 1931, and for years graced the office of oil mogul Armand Hammer on the 78th floor of the Empire State Building. Its return to Uxbridge followed a visit by the then Princess Elizabeth, who, on a visit to New York, expressed an interest in it. The gallant Dr Hammer gave it to her as a Coronation present, and she had it restored to its original setting.

No-one knows when the house became an inn, but it was well-known

by 1819 when it was bought by the Marlow brewer Wethered's, now part of Whitbread, and perhaps it was first licensed when the coach road went through in 1785. It was definitely an inn soon after, for it has a Parliament clock. These date to 1797 when Parliament taxed clocks to pay for the wars with France, and most citizens could not afford their own. Publicans bought them to tempt in those who simply wanted to know the time but might also feel constrained to buy a drink.

OPEN *all permitted hours*
STATION *Uxbridge BR*
BEERS *Whitbread range*
FOOD *meals & snacks lunchtime & evening*
Garden

KING'S ARMS
LION GATES, HAMPTON COURT RD, KT9

Hampton Court with its maze is one of London's most popular and historic tourist attractions, and the King's Arms makes a worthy book-end to the palace's magnificent Lion Gates.

Hampton was not much of a place when the Ipswich butcher's son made good, Cardinal Thomas Wolsey, Archbishop of York, chose it as the site for his splendid home in 1515. But if it was only a hamlet on a boggy turn of the Thames a good stiff row from London itself, it did have one vital recommendation: it was scarcely a flattering whisper away from Richmond Palace, now gone, but then the favoured seat of Henry VIII.

Wolsey's failure to get Henry's barren marriage to Katherine of Aragon annulled turned the King against him. The gift of Hampton Court did nothing to allay the royal ire (although it did spell ruin for Richmond Palace); and Wolsey was lucky to die of natural causes in 1530, aged 55, before the headsman could have a hack at him.

The King's Arms at Hampton Court's imperial Lion Gates is a worthy inn for such a setting. It has been refreshing visitors to the palace for two centuries or thereabouts, its white-painted, bow-windowed frontage speaking unmistakably of the late 18th century.

Inside, the aura is that of the coaching inn, even if the pitch has always been more at

pleasure-trippers than at genuine travellers. The three principal rooms, lined up along an imposing front, include a bareboards spit-and-sawdust public bar; a slightly more formal room whose black panelling may or may not be the genuine article but conveys the genuine atmosphere; and a large dining-room with blue mosaic floor-tiles of uncertain provenance. Vaguely period bric-a-brac, including yellowing bills for coal and suchlike, enhance the pub's persona.

Lately the neighbouring building has been incorporated as a bakery and bistro. The addition has been part of a widely welcomed facelift for the old inn.

OPEN *all permitted hours*
STATION *Hampton Court BR*
BEERS *Hall & Woodhouse range*
FOOD *meals & snacks lunchtime & evening*
Restaurant
Garden

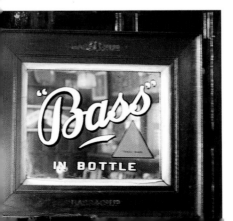

THE PRINCE ALFRED
FORMOSA ST, W9

A very well-preserved but rather scruffy survivor from 1863, the Prince Alfred is something of an architectural marvel, combining almost every feature characteristic of the times and being almost an object-lesson in glass and mahogany.

The front is remarkable enough: it's actually open, the entire weight of the upper floors being supported via lintels supported on impossibly slim iron columns with a slight barleysugar twist to them. The windows, structurally, are no more than screens: bearing no loads, they are free to curve and convolute as they wish, the elegantly sculpted mahogany frames forming arches and oriels around the gloriously etched plate-glass.

The standard lamps on the kerb outside, now rather truncated, are also part of the pub; not placed there by the municipality for the safety of the citizens, but by the landlord for the advertisement of the Prince Alfred.

Inside, five private bars, separated from each other by glass and mahogany partitions, are grouped around the high, ornate bar-wagon. One of these, originally for women only, retains its pivoting snob-screens.

A remarkable feature of these private bars is that they are accessible only through tiny doors no more than 3' 6" tall, so unless you want to remain in the rather dingy billiard room at the back, you have to be prepared to look foolish.

Actually, each of the private bars has its own street door, and originally these were the usual means of access, while the little hatches in the partitions were really intended for the cleaners. In a similar pub in Hull once, a man robbed a customer in one such private bar and made his escape via the

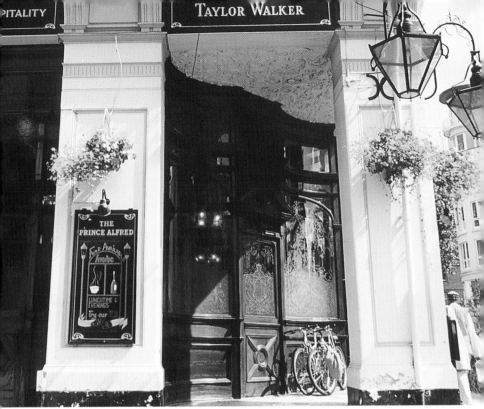

hatches, "running like a rat all round the pub", according to a witness. For some reason, all the street doors at the Prince Alfred are kept locked except the one in the magnificently-tiled principal lobby.

The pub is named after Queen Victoria's second son, who was made Duke of Edinburgh in 1862 and at the same time turned down an offer from Greece to become King of the Hellenes.

OPEN *all permitted hours*
STATION *Warwick Avenue tube*
BEERS *Carlsberg-Tetley range*
FOOD *meals & snacks lunchtime*

THE VICTORIA & ALBERT
MARYLEBONE STATION, NW1

There's not a trace of melamine or tile-effect flooring in sight at this most magnificent of London station buffets. Instead, there's ornate plaster, polished mahogany, and acres of plate glass in a pair of bars that rival the grandest of 1890s gin-palaces.

So why should the builders of the station have gone to town in quite such a degree? The answer lies in Paris. Marylebone Station was the last of main London termini. It was built between 1891 and 1897 as the London end of a branch of the Manchester Sheffield & Lincoln Railway, originally known simply as the MSL London Extension, but rechristened the Great Central Railway by its dour and ambitious proprietor, Sir Edward Watkin.

Sir Edward, a Mancunian who had pioneered the London Underground as chairman of the Metropolitan railway, was also a director of the London & South-Eastern Railway and had extensive business interests on the Continent. His grand plan was to merge them all with the creation of a direct line from Manchester to Paris – as part of which he envisaged the digging of a Channel tunnel.

So confident was he that he even built the line to the greater loading potential normal on the Continent. But it never happened. Railway politics – Sir Edward was widely hated – prevented the building of the tunnel (which was probably well within the technical grasp of the engineers of the day); Marylebone never became the hub of international commerce and communications that he planned; before long, even its links to the north fell into disuse thanks to the existence of other, more convenient lines; eventually the line closed altogether beyond Amersham, and Marylebone became the most luxurious and under-used commuter terminus in the world.

But the grandeur lingers on. Of the two bars which make up the Victoria & Albert, the first has been rather unsympathetically redecorated; but the second and larger room retains the grandeur of the Victorian dining room it was originally intended to be.

Above the picture rail, plaster nymphs disport; below, huge plate-glass mirrors shine; the big fireplaces are all mahogany and marble; and what with its dark panelling and wallpaper, the room feels more like the reading-room of a gentleman's club than a common-or-garden station buffet.

The Victoria & Albert has become a haven of quiet and a rare outlet for independent brewers' beers.

OPEN *11-11 mon-fri, 11-9.30 sat*
STATION *need you ask?*
BEERS *from independent brewers*

THE WARRINGTON
93 WARRINGTON CRESCENT, W9

This is a plump, blowsy madame of a pub, all red carpets and plaster cherubs; and indeed, they do say that in its heyday when it was a hotel, a lot more went on in the letting rooms than strictly should have. Built in the 1850s but entirely remodelled in the early years of this century, the Warrington sits at the meeting-point of a number of extremely affluent residential streets. But there's nothing reticent about the Warrington: it's not one of those demure little servants' pubs hiding discreetly down some half-concealed mews.

Indeed, its frontage is quite as palatial as any of the adjoining mansions, and far more florid. Mosaic steps lead up to a portico with faience pillars and tiles from Ironbridge in Shropshire. Inside, the opulent grandeur is unrestrained: there's black oak in profusion, a marble bar-counter, floral ceiling, and glass of all sorts – brilliant-cut, acid-etched and painted as well.

Was it really ever a brothel? Possibly, but unlikely. Brothels on the pattern of the French maison tolerée were always unusual in England, and the Criminal Law Amendment Act of 1885 swept away the few there were. It may be, though, that the Warrington was a so-called accommodation house, where a woman could take a client for an hour and pay pro rata in return, perhaps, for a cut of the take or the guaranteed purchase of a few drinks before going upstairs.

Certainly, the place had a reputation: the music-hall star Marie Lloyd was a regular, and by all accounts a great toper of champagne. Long after its Edwardian heyday, it did its best to maintain the air: at one time it sported a neon-sign proclaiming it "the liveliest lounge in London"; and the slightly risqué murals around the bar and window in the lounge look to me like later additions – 30s, perhaps – interpolated to enhance the Warrington's naughty image.

What made all this the more piquant was that until it was sold to its sitting tenants in 1983 the Warrington stood slap-bang in the middle of

one of the two great Church Commission estates in London, whose rents paid the livings of Church of England clergy. The irony of the nation's vicars living, at least in part, on immoral earnings, lent authenticity to the Warrington's past as a brothel – even if only as the result of wishful thinking.

OPEN *all permitted hours*
STATION *Warwick Avenue tube*
BEERS *Fuller's, Young's, Marston's, guests*
FOOD *meals & snacks lunchtime & evening*

THE WARWICK CASTLE

6 WARWICK PLACE, W9

There is nothing particularly historic about this quiet local, but to sit here quietly for a while with a glass of cool London Pride is the most practical way of learning one very important thing about London's pubs and their history: why people liked them so much.

Warwick Place is a quiet and elegant little cul-de-sac on the fringe of that most delicious of enclaves, Little Venice. Scarcely a hundred yards from the pub's front door, broad and busy streets of spacious villas front the canal and its colourful fringe of brightly-painted narrow-boats. But here all is calm: a permanent Sunday in a city of Monday mornings.

The Warwick is no grand gin-palace; nor is it a hoary and ancient tavern of the sort where, you just know, Dr Johnson, Goldsmith, Steele, Garrick,

Gainsborough and the whole battalion of 18th-century bon viveurs once traded quips over a bottle of sack.

It's just a pub, dating maybe to the 1850s, its walls lined with simple matchboarding, embellished with touches of fine glass in the lobby and the top bar-fitting, with a cute little marble fireplace in a cute little snug.

OPEN *all permitted hours*
STATION *Warwick Avenue tube*
BEERS *Bass range plus guests*
FOOD *meals & snacks lunchtime, snacks evening*

THE WINDSOR CASTLE
114 CAMPDEN HILL RD, W8

Anyone who is accustomed to the melancholy roll-call of lovely old pubs that have been "improved" and "refurbished" beyond all recognition wonders how such a marvellous mid-Victorian relic can have been permitted to survive.

As one who generally prefers the cock-up theory to the conspiracy theory, I suspect that the Windsor Castle has remained as it is more through the brewery's neglect than through its reverence for history. Fortunately we have arrived at a more sensitive time: the brewery has woken up to the potential of the place as it is, and one can say with some confidence that short of natural catastrophe – Campden Hill turning out to be volcanic, say – the pub's unaltered future is secure.

The area was laid out in the 1840s, before which it was a rolling country district of farm and park speckled with substantial houses such as Norland House, whose memory now only survives in Norland Square; Holland House and its Park; and the Earl of Nottingham's house on the very edge of Kensington, taken over by William and Mary in 1688 and rebuilt by Wren as Kensington Palace.

The Windsor Castle is supposed to have got its name because, before the area was thoroughly developed, you could see the Castle from its upstairs windows. Is this true, I wonder, of London's 16 other pubs of the same name? The pub is still divided by partitions of dark wood and acid-etched glass into its three original separate bars, each with its own street-entrance; to pass between them you have to use little hatches not much larger than those at the Prince Alfred in Maida Vale, originally

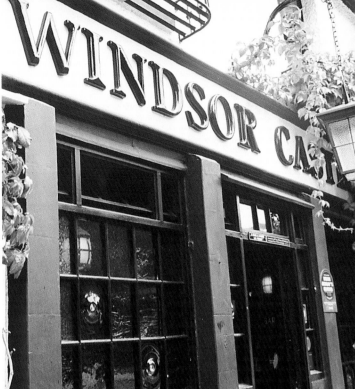

meant for the cleaners.

As well as the three front bars, with their high-backed settles forming little alcoves, their dark wood panelling, and their bare floorboards, there is also the Sherry Bar at the back, where the fashionable drink is a Huntsman, a Bloody Mary made with fino sherry instead of vodka; and the large stone-flagged garden with its shady London plane tree. It is a wonderful place in which to raise a glass to years of neglect.

OPEN *all permitted hours*
STATION *Notting Hill Gate tube*
BEERS *Bass ales*
FOOD *meals & snacks lunchtime & evening*
Garden

AROUND THE HEATH

Highgate and Hampstead, perched on hills on either side of the Heath, have managed, despite having been engulfed by London's vast sprawling mass, to retain something of their village charm, remaining oases of relative calm amid the hectic pace of the rest of the capital.

In the 18th and 19th centuries both villages were a vital source of spring water to cholera-ravaged London. People would come in droves bearing leather flasks to collect the water. Two pubs, one in either village, both named the Flask, serve as a reminder to those times and the tradition of imbibing there continues to this day – although now the tired and thirsty Londoner is more likely to relax over a pint than a flask of water.

Hampstead, originally a more proletarian enclave, is most famous these days as home to London's intelligentsia. Highgate may not attract as many of the living literary elite, but it compensates by housing London's most famous graveyard, Highgate cemetery, which includes among its graves those of Christina Rosetti and George Eliot.

Above The Freemasons – an oasis by the heath

FREEMASONS ARMS
32 DOWNSHIRE HILL, NW3

Is Downshire Hill the most beautiful residential street in London? If such a palm were awarded it would make for hard judging; but this elegant street with its exclusive mansions and picturesque cottages, sloping gently down from Rosslyn Hill and the quaint centre of Hampstead to Hampstead Ponds and beyond them the Heath, would surely be a strong contender.

The mansions and cottages are for the most part very early 19th century, and the original Freemasons was built at about the same time, complete with a pell mell court (pell mell was an early version of croquet which was at its most popular in the 17th century) which still survives.

The original pub also had an alley for London skittles, a variant in which a 12lb flat, round "cheese" of lignum vitae was pitched at the hornbeam pins, rather than rolled as in the more common West Country version. The Freemasons still has its skittle alley, one of only a handful of London alleys in existence; and it sees plenty of use, too.

The present Freemasons, however, is scarcely 60 years old: the original was found to be unsafe during a survey in the mid 1930s and had to be demolished and replaced.

Pubs of the 1930s have been deprecated for a long time, and not just because they were, until recently, too new to get nostalgic about: a conscious move away from both the excesses of the Victorian gin-palace and the unsophistication of the rustic beer-house started just before the First World War; but these virtues are back in fashion now, and the "improved" pubs of the 1920s and 30s have been under appreciated.

The Freemasons, though, is something special. A conscious attempt to reinterpret the "Queen Anne" style of the 1850s and '60s, its large airy spaces have the cool elegance demanded by the pub's setting.

It is essentially one large room, broken up by high-back settles and wood and glass partitions, but with the distinction that the wood here is pale, rather than the black oak favoured by the Victorians. One end is all bare timber, while the other is pale stained panelling and chintzy furniture, and there's a third area at the back used for dining.

The calm sophistication with which the architects handled this large space begs a question: why are the pub designers of today so obsessed with mock-Victoriana? A visit to the Freemasons would give them new ideas.

OPEN *all permitted hours*
STATIONS *Hampstead Heath BR & Hampstead tube*
BEERS *Bass range*
FOOD *meals & snacks lunchtime & evening*
Garden

FLASK TAVERN
14 FLASK WALK, NW3

In the 18th century, London was expanding fast as new inhabitants poured in from the countryside. Unfortunately, its infrastructure was nowhere near keeping up with the influx, and as a result the older quarters were degenerating into seething, stinking, crime-ridden slums with neither adequate means of sewage and garbage disposal nor reliable sources of clean water.

One source of relief for the denizens of the Great Wen was to walk or, if they were affluent enough, drive out of the city whenever possible to take advantage of the countless tea-houses, pleasure-gardens and, from the middle of the 18th century, mineral spas that were beginning to spring up all around.

The Albion and the Eagle in Islington, the Angel in Bermondsey and the other Flask, in Highgate, are all associated with this trade in pleasure-trippers, and so is the Flask in Hampstead. Before Hampstead's springs were adjudged to have medicinal properties, the pub that stood here was called the Thatched House; its new name referred to and advertised its trade in bottled spring water. (Not that all its habitués were there for the water, mind: the novelist Samuel Richardson refers in *Clarissa* to Hampstead as "a place where second-rate characters are to be found, occasionally in swinish condition".)

Despite its present high social standing, Hampstead evolved in the 19th century as a working-class area, and many of the houses which now command such astronomical prices are clearly no more than artisan's cottages. The Flask developed as a working-class alehouse; and even when it was rebuilt in 1873 it was on a fairly humble scale – apart from a few glazed tiles, its facade could almost be called plain.

The present layout and decorative scheme seems to have been added later, since the painted panels dividing the two front bars are dated 1880 and appear to have been manufactured in Paris. But this is not one of the great ornate fantasies of the 90s: the comparatively unadorned joinery

and tiled dado in the public bar belong to a respectable, low-key workers' alehouse. Since the war, Hampstead's once-proletarian lanes and alleys have filled up with writers, artists, musicians and actors, who have made the Flask a favourite watering-hole. But it is still welcoming to less elevated locals, and there is nothing high-faluting about its decor or atmosphere. The dining rooms at the rear were added only in 1990 but manage not to jar.

OPEN *all permitted hours*
STATION *Hampstead tube*
BEERS *Young's range*
FOOD *meals & snacks lunchtime & evening*
Disabled access.

Above The Flask – Parisian panelling in a proletarian pub

HOLLY BUSH
22 HOLLY MOUNT, NW3

This has to be one of the strangest little pubs in London. An odd mix of country inn and city tavern, it suits the mood of its rus-in-urbe enclave perfectly.

Holly Mount is itself a curiously higgledy-piggledy part of Hampstead, with tall narrow houses and once-humble cottages crowding into each other in a maze of narrow little alleys, stairs, and walkways more akin to Clovelly or Whitby than to one of the most fashionable residential areas of a great capital city.

The pub was built in 1643, but not as a pub. It was in fact the stable-

Above The timeless interior of the Holly Bush

block of the house at the back, which was for a short while from 1796 the home of the painter George Romney.

Romney moved here from Cavendish Square, Bayswater, to get away from it all; and in particular to get away from Lady Hamilton, with whom he was miserably obsessed and whom he kept painting in a variety of Classical – and nude – allegorical scenes. He soon found he hadn't got far away enough and moved to Kendal in the Lake District, where he died in 1802.

A few years after his flight from fantasy, in about 1807 in fact, his house was converted into the local Assembly Rooms, with the old stables adapted as the catering block, housing kitchens, beer-stores, and servants' quarters. Not long after, the Assembly Rooms became the Hampstead Literary & Scientific Society, and the stables-turned-kitchens became the Holly Bush.

A fairly modest exterior gives way to a truly remarkable and completely unspoilt front bar: pure proletarian high-backed settles, bare floors, matchboard-clad walls, and smoke-darkened low ceilings are offset by odd bits and pieces of high-'90s glasswork and moulding, as if a landlord of 100 years ago had saved his pennies and imported as many of the hottest items as he could afford – even incorporating the '90s fashion for privacy by hiving off each end of the bar to form a pair of cosy snugs.

The pub has lost nothing of that characteristic cheek-by-jowl blend of proletarian and bourgeois which typifies Hampstead: it definitely belongs to Hampstead's working-class past, but it's wearing every scrap of finery it owns – like Giles's Gran answering the door to the rentman in her nightie and foxfur stole.

OPEN *12-3, 5-11 mon-fri,*
12-4, 6-11 sat, 12-3, 7-10.30 sun
STATION *Hampstead tube*
BEERS *Carlsberg-Tetley range*
FOOD *Meals & snacks lunchtime (not mon)*

THE OLD BULL & BUSH

NORTH END RD, NW3

On the strength of a single theatrical song, the Old Bull & Bush proclaims itself as the most famous pub in London; but even if the Australian-born music-hall star Florrie Ford had never brought it such celebrity, it would still rank as one of London's great inns. Built in 1645 as a farm, the Bull & Bush was first recorded as an inn in 1721, when Hampstead was just beginning to come into fashion as a conveniently-located and picturesque place of resort for well-heeled Londoners. Indeed many of the richest of them chose to live here, with great houses such as North End House, where Pitt the Elder resided briefly in a vain effort to regain his health.

The painter Hogarth was one of the Bull & Bush's earliest high-society patrons, planting a yew bower at the back in which he could paint in peace. Later in the century the actor David Garrick and the painters Reynolds and Gainsborough called in on a day out, prompting Gainsborough to comment: "What a delightful little snuggery is this Bull & Bush."

The pub lost nothing of its celebrity in the following century, when Dickens, Wilkie Collins, George du Maurier and other media types would take their ease here on days out from the pernicious air of the City.

However in 1867 it changed its aim somewhat when the landlord added extensive pleasure gardens, which proved a magnet to the more workaday trippers right up until World War I. Certainly the "little German band" of which 15-stone Florrie Ford trilled in 1903 would not have been welcome 11 years later!

As so often happens, the Bull & Bush's greatest moment was also its last moment of greatness, for many years at least. In 1907 the tube arrived, enabling even more Londoners to take a day trip to its gardens. At its peak it attracted 700 of them a day. At the same time the area to the north began to be developed, creating a huge population where before there had been none – but then came the War, and with it a

drastic reduction in business.

After the War, the owner, Ind Coope, sought to revive the pub's fortunes with a great rebuilding programme, which in 1923 saw part of the gardens turned into a car-park – doubtless to attract the car-owning middle classes of the new suburbs – and the ancient Stuart farmhouse massively extended.

A further investment of £400,000 in the early 1980s extended it still further; and if it is not quite as popular yet as it was in Florrie Ford's day, it is still as famous. And yet it retains an air of the 18th century, with intimate little bays and alcoves in dark wood and nicotine plaster, and a large airy extension to one side conveying the atmosphere of a Georgian country-house library.

OPEN *all permitted hours*
STATION *Golders Green or Hampstead tube*
BEERS *Carlsberg-Tetley range plus guests*
FOOD *Restaurant*
Gardens

Above The Old Bull & Bush

THE SPANIARD'S INN
SPANIARD'S RD, NW3

A degree of controversy surrounds the name of this splendid old pub. Were the Spaniards in question the Spanish Ambassador and his entourage in the days of James I, whose country residence this allegedly was? Or were they two Spanish brothers, who supposedly converted the building into a pub in the mid-18th century and fought a memorable duel over a women, who then sensibly spurned the pair of them?

You pays your money and you takes your choice with stories like these; but at least they are not mutually exclusive. The latter tale, however, does exclude any association with Dick Turpin, whose leg-irons, keys, and pistols are on show at the pub (or were, until someone nicked the pistols): Turpin had his neck stretched at York in 1739, while the hot-tempered Latin brothers are not supposed to have arrived on the scene until a few years later.

Does it matter? Not really. Anthropologists call these kind of stories charter-myths, and what matters is not whether you can prove but whether they enhance your appreciation of the pub. Which they usually do.

One story that does have the ring of truth is that during the Gordon Riots of 1780 the landlord, Giles Thomas, saved Kenwood House from being torched by a mob on the pretext that it belonged to a peer who didn't mind Catholics. Thomas, feigning sympathy, plied the rioters with liquor until the cavalry arrived.

A story that is definitely fictitious is that of Dickens' Mrs Bardell who was arrested in the garden here while taking tea with friends, having failed to pay the costs of her breach of promise suit against Mr Pickwick.

Whether the Spaniards had any stories or not, it would still be one of the most atmospheric pubs in London. It has the requisite bare floorboards, black oak panels and partitions, and nicotine plaster. It also has a smashing little snug at the back, a dining room to one side, another room upstairs, and a tiny porch-room which will seat nine thin people who don't mind touching.

The little blockhouse across the road which creates a dangerous bottleneck and ought to be demolished can't be, because it is an 18th-century toll-keeper's cottage and is listed. And anyway, Dick Turpin stabled Black Bess in it, so there.

OPEN *all permitted hours*
STATION *Hampstead tube (but it's a long slog: try a 210 bus)*
BEERS *Bass range plus guests*
FOOD *meals & snacks lunchtime; snacks evening*
Restaurant, garden

THE FLASK
77, HIGHGATE WEST HILL, N6

Some say there has been an inn on the site since the reign of Henry VI, although 1663 is the date more usually given for the genesis of this fine old inn. Certainly the rambling interior layout, with its ups and downs, its snugs and alcoves have a 17th-century feel about them, for all the pleasant Georgian classicism of the mellow brick front and its cobbled courtyard, which belong to 1767.

The Highgate Flask, with its air of squirearchical solidity, is much posher than its Hampstead namesake. What they have in common is that in the 18th century they were both associated with spas – with the springs, in fact, from which rose the twin sources of the Fleet – supplying bottles in which pilgrims could trap the precious curative waters.

Now you may not think that the water in either Hampstead Ponds or Highgate Ponds looks particularly healthful; but the medicinal claims made for them in the 18th century were accurate at least in the sense that these waters would not kill you, which their sewage-laden lower reaches almost certainly would.

The Flask is yet another London pub which claims Dick Turpin for its own – in this case, he is reported as having hidden in the cellars. It's unlikely. For one thing, Turpin and his gang spent more of their time terrorising Epping Forest than Hampstead Heath; for another, the kind of pub which would give Turpin refuge would more likely be some low beerhouse or dramshop, especially one with a sideline in receiving stolen goods, than a prosperous establishment resort such as this.

(Actually Dick Turpin, the psychopathic son of an Essex butcher, was as much a housebreaker as a highwaymen and was not very nice: he once broke into the home of an old widow and sat her on the fire until she told him where the money was. Very romantic).

The Flask remained fashionable throughout the 18th and 19th centuries, attracting Hogarth (who got a good beating in a brawl his own companions had started and which he, bizarrely, attempted to sketch);

Morland, a great artist in both senses of the word; Cruikshank before he became a rabid teetotaller in the 1840s; and the impoverished Karl Marx whenever he had the capital.

Extensive refurbishments in 1910 and 1993 have done nothing to spoil the near-rural character of this most eminent of London's country inns.

No description of the Flask is complete without reference to the cod-antique "swearing the horns" ceremony, in which the initiate kisses antlers tied to pole and vows never to touch small beer when strong ale is available and never to kiss the maid when the mistress is about, but rather than miss the chance kiss them both. This grisly procedure bears the masculine stamp of the suburban golf club or minor masonic lodge; but it has a long history: Byron refers to it, and some people think it goes back to the Restoration.

OPEN *all permitted hours*
STATION *Highgate tube*
BEERS *Carlsberg-Tetley range plus guests*
FOOD *meals & snacks lunchtime & evening*
Garden

NORTH LONDON

North London has clearer geographical delineations, and hence a more obvious character, than the capital's other three quarters, mainly because of the dominating scarp of Hornsey, Highgate and Hampstead. It was from Highgate Hill that Dick Whittington turned, saw the City spread glittering before him, and could not resist going back for one more try.

As the pubs around Hampstead Heath have been given their own separate chapter, we concentrate here on a similar crawl around Islington. The other pubs range as far north as The Fallow Buck in Enfield and the Phoenix at Alexandra Palace, which offers stunning views across almost every pub roof in north London.

Islington is an archetype of the north London working-class suburb. Originally pasture land, it was developed in the 19th century to provide housing for the booming population of city clerks and itinerant

labourers who would walk to their jobs in the City or constructing the railways. The area became seedy and run down in the post-war era but is now the increasingly middle-class and gentrified home of the well-to-do. Many of the pubs are Victorian in origin, built to serve a thirsty working population and serving still.

Above The panoramic view from the Phoenix at Alexandra Palace

THE ALBION

10 THORNHILL RD, N1

SUCH a dignified late Georgian quarter of North London deserves a dignified late Georgian pub, and in the Albion it has a perfect example. A big countrified pub, the Albion has the dimensions, the apartments, and the grandeur of a notable coaching inn – which is perhaps why it claims to have been just that.

Alas, it never was. Everything is against the claim. Thornhill Street has never been a coach route, for one thing: it was shown as a muddy lane through market gardens on a parish map of 1805, when what is now the Albion was first marked as a tea-room. The coaches went up Liverpool Road, a few degrees to the east.

Then there is the total lack of stables, or of any evidence that any ever existed. They cannot have stood behind the pub, because that was a pound used by geese being driven from East Anglia to the London markets. If they were in front of the pub, across the road, as stables sometimes were, they are not marked on the early map.

In fact, the Albion's roots lie in the days before London's great Victorian explosion, the days when the city was

still compact enough for its people to stroll out on a fine evening to take their ease in tranquil and picturesque areas of near-countryside. The Albion has never known the hustle and bustle of the great commercial inn; it has always been a place of leisure pure and simple, and none the worse for it.

It still is. As perfect in its proportions as Albion Lodge next door but one and the charming villas in Ripplevale Lane hard by, the Albion is the ideal watering hole for the affluent and civilised people of the district.

Inside, a grand front bar leads into magnificent back rooms, one elegant, one with something of a Washington Irving inn-kitchen feel, right down to the stone-flagged floor. Beyond again lies one of the best pub gardens in London: part-roofed by a great vine-covered pergola, the garden is large and plain, but such a place of refuge that you could easily imagine yourself in the Cotswolds.

OPEN *all permitted hours*
STATION *Caledonian Rd BR, Highbury tube*
BEERS *ScottishCourage range*
FOOD *meals & snacks lunchtime & evening*
Garden

THE CAMDEN HEAD

CAMDEN PASSAGE, N1

For years this dignified and handsome pub has been the local for the stallholders of Camden Passage antiques market, and as a result it has an authentic atmosphere which tourists love. But it's a fine pub, dating to the great pub-building boom of the late 1890s and, rarely, sensitively restored in the callous and cavalier 1960s.

There has been a pub on the site since 1806, but the present confection of pink brick with pale stone strings, windows, and medallions was built, as a plaque records, in 1899 – the very last year, as it happens, of London's great boom in pub-building. Inside, the partition screens have, as is so tragically common, all been removed to create one large but cosy bar arranged around an island whose bar-wagon and clock survive, along with a fair jumble of original woodwork and acid-etched glass.

The Camden Head is very lucky in the care taken in its last major remodelling in 1969, a period when pubs of this vintage tended to be vandalised. In this case, however, pieces of the original partitions were reused to form alcoves, and to restore the upstairs room glass was even brought in from a contemporary house in West London which was being demolished at a time when, in other pubs, ornately brilliant-cut and acid-etched glasswork was being smashed and discarded by the acre.

The Camden Head is not only a handsome pub well-sited for explorers of Islington's delights; it is also an example of how a pub that was designed for the needs of a past age can be adapted for the needs of today without being wrecked in the process.

OPEN *all permitted hours*
STATION *Angel tube*
BEERS *ScottishCourage range*
FOOD *full meals & snacks lunchtime*
Terrace

CROCKER'S FOLLY
24, ABERDEEN PLACE, NW8.

HERE is true folly: folly preserved forever in mahogany and marble, folly on a princely scale, folly so tragic that London has been laughing about it for over a century. Originally the Crown Hotel, this grand pub was built in the 1890s in an unassuming Maida Vale side-street by a Kilburn publican named Frank Crocker. And what a palace Frank built!

It had – still has – two bars: a public bar of no more than ordinary magnificence, and a grand saloon with marble bar-top and pilasters, marble stringing, marble archways, even a great marble fireplace; with a magnificent Jacobean-style coffered ceiling of the most intricate plasterwork; and acres of gleaming woodwork.

It is mad – the demented dream of an architect who has overdosed on a mixture of hallucinogens and mason's catalogues. The former billiard-room, now a carvery, is scarcely less ornate: but perhaps the bust of Caracalla is a sly demonstration that the pub's designers were quite conscious of the excesses to which their client was pushing them: Caracalla was a Roman emperor known for his architectural excesses and his complete insanity.

The whole thing was the biggest gamble in the history of pubs: the railway was approaching from the north, heading straight as an arrow for Maida Vale. Surely, reasoned Crocker, it would stop right where he was building his palatial pub; and the Crown Hotel would become the Railway Hotel, and a goldmine.

Alas for Crocker! The line turned left a few degrees at St John's Wood, to terminate not at his doorway, but about a mile away, where Marylebone Station now

stands. The Crown Hotel was a palace in the middle of nowhere; the grandest folie in London.

Crocker, naturally, went bust and then killed himself by jumping out of an upstairs window.

For years the pub mouldered on as an absurdly grand local; a photograph of 1967 shows it much as it was built, even down to a few surviving sticks of the original custom-made furniture. Only the gas-fittings had been changed, and the tawdry little lights with which they had been replaced speak volumes.

In 1983 the Crown was bought by north-eastern brewer Vaux, which formally adopted its nickname and then sold it to Regent Inns, which now runs it at a big, bustling, profit. They say Crocker's ghost appears each evening at cashing-up time, his dead eyes bulging with spectral envy.

OPEN *all permitted hours*
STATION *Warwick Ave, Edgware Rd tube*
BEERS *nine, including Brakspear, Adnams, Gale's*
FOOD *meals lunchtime & evening*

THE EAGLE TAVERN
2 SHEPHERDESS WALK, N1

This, as it doesn't tire of boasting, is the Eagle Tavern of Pop Goes The Weasel fame. Or is it? In fact the site has a long and complex history, and the pub you see today is in some ways but a footnote. The song itself dates in recognisable form to about 1780, although it seems to have older roots. Ambiguous in detail, it's abundantly clear in meaning, for while the "weasel" is variously defined as a colloquialism for a tailor's flat-iron or a leather-worker's punch, there's no mistaking the meaning of the word "pop": it meant, and still means, to pawn. Underpaid Victorian craftsmen, in whatever industry they worked, habitually pawned their tools to buy drink, and publicans were glad to be uncle in the transaction.

As for the Eagle, it rose to prominence in 1825 when it was bought along with the adjoining fields by one Thomas Rouse, to create one of the many pleasure gardens which surrounded London and which were places of mass entertainment with food, drink, music, dancing, loose women and all the other delights that the inhabitants of a great city will pay good money for.

In 1831 a music-hall, the Moorish Pavilion, was built alongside; and in 1840 the whole pub was rebuilt on a grand scale worthy of "the statuary, the garden orchestra, the fountains, the gas devices, the brilliant illuminations of variegated lamps in stars, wreaths, and mottos; the beautifully-painted cosmoramas, the set scenes, the magic mirrors, the Olympic Temple, the saloon, the double band, the great French rope-dancers, the infant prodigies, the grotesque brothers, select vaudevilles, laughable ballets, and the peculiar extravaganza the pas de coco, together with a first-rate concert of vocal instrumental music" boasted in Rouse's advertising material.

Shortly after that it was licensed as a theatre, the Grecian, which attracted all the great names of the mid-Victorian stage. The theatre licence, required by all "proper" auditoriums under the 1843 Theatres

Up and down the City Road
In and out the Eagle
Thats the way the money goes
Pop! goes the Weasel

SHEPHERDESS
PLACE

THE EAGLE

Act, proved a pretension too far, though, for it forbade smoking and drinking in the auditorium; and in 1882 both the Grecian and the Eagle went bust, were bought up by the Salvation Army, and demolished to make way for a hostel and citadel.

Perhaps the site was jinxed, for not only did the hostel and citadel never materialise, but somehow the licence was never suppressed, and in 1900 an entirely new pub was built on the site – the Eagle that you see today.

Only one tiled entrance lobby, the outline of the bar, and half-a-dozen pale green marble columns survive of the original decor, but the Eagle is a large, pleasant, airy pub with a secluded beer-garden, and a very welcome refuge from the noise and fumes of today's City Road. Sadly, though, no laughable ballet.

OPEN *all permitted hours*
STATION *Old Street tube*
BEERS *Bass & Highgate ales*
FOOD *meals & snacks lunchtime & evening*

THE FALLOW BUCK

CLAY HILL, ENFIELD

It's hard to believe that this ancient country pub with its hill-top setting and breathtaking views over to Epping Forest is actually in London. And indeed it wasn't until 1965, if the campaign to restore Middlesex to its former status as a county ever succeeds, it won't be any more.

The building has been dated to 1674 thanks to the discovery of a plaque, probably left by a plasterer – although it could well be older – and used to be the very last building in the straggling hamlet of Clay Hill before the gates of the huge Royal Forest of Enfield Chase.

The Chase was set aside as a hunting preserve to supply both sport and meat for the royal household soon after the Norman conquest. A passion for hunting seems to have been in the genes of all the dynasties from Norman to Tudor, and monarchs from William II to Elizabeth I were personally familiar with the coverts and spinneys of Enfield Chase.

The more effete Stuarts, however, cared little for hunting, and through the 17th and 18th centuries Enfield Chase became a byword for misman-agement, the worst poachers being the verderers themselves. One can't help wondering whether the Fallow Buck, being the nearest habitation, also proved the handiest emporium for their ill-gotten venison.

In 1777 the royal household decided that ownership of such a dodgy asset was neither use nor ornament, and had much of the area enclosed. The Fallow Buck has been an inn since at least this time; it's marked as such on a map of 1822, but its regulars by then will have been more interested in lettuce than deer, for the district became an important centre for market-gardening, supplying the capital's ever-growing demand for fresh fruit and vegetables. The area still has more than its fair share of nurseries and garden centres, direct descendants of the horticul-

turists of two centuries ago. The surviving stretches of the old Chase are also important centres for outdoor pursuits of all types: golf; walking; and above all, in a faint echo of the past, riding – the pub even has a hitching rail in its car park.

The Fallow Buck's antiquity is evident from its construction: it is timber-framed and weatherboarded, a method of construction common in Essex and once just as common in Middlesex, although Enfield today has few surviving examples. Inside, some of the original alcoves and snugs have been preserved among the 17th-century oak studding and joists, giving the pub an atmosphere to match its age and setting.

OPEN *11-2.30 6-11 mon-wed, 11-3.30 6-11 thur-sat, 12-10.30 sun.*
STATIONS *Gordon Hill BR, Crew Hill BR*
FOOD *meals & snacks lunchtime & evening*
Restaurant

THE ISLAND QUEEN
87 NOEL RD, N1

The Island Queen is a fixture in every guide-book there is; yet at heart it's a fine but unexceptional late Victorian pub in an attractive and affluent but unexceptional residential street.

But Noel Road wasn't always so attractive and so affluent: in the 1960s it was, like much of Islington, run-down and raffish, the houses broken up into bed-sits and flats where poor artists lived cheek-by-jowl with working-class families. It was in one of these houses that the playwright Joe Orton and his lover Kenneth Halliwell lived and, through Halliwell's paranoid jealousy, died. But that's not why the Island Queen is famous. Nor is it famous on architectural grounds: a fair few original features survive – a carved bar-back, and some glass bar-screens at eye-level, the fore-runners of the louvered snob screens. But it's hardly on a level with the capital's great Victorian survivals such as the Princess Louise or the Argyll.

No, what people like so much about the Island Queen is that it's a paradigm of Englishness. It's an antique, but not self-consciously so. It's comfortable, cosy, slightly scuffed. And it's completely barking mad.

Madness in the form of dioramas depicting 18th-century piracy mounted on rickety galleries overhead; life-size dummies dressed up as pirates complete with wooden legs fence with rapiers and fire a cannon amid a tangle of rigging. There is a furled sail and, at ground level, a huge and very genuine-looking figurehead.

It's all a fairly recent feature and there's nothing even remotely nautical in the Island Queen's past. Yet the

pirates lend a quirky charm without swamping the pub's original qualities. Retaining its gin palace-style open plan and large front windows, it has a pleasant, airy atmosphere (especially in Summer when sunlight streams in), making it a great place for a quiet drink away from the bustle of Islington's main thoroughfares.

OPEN *12-3 5.30-11 mon-sat, 12-3, 5.30-10.30 sun*
STATION *Angel tube*
BEERS *Bass, Greene King, Fuller's range*
FOOD *meals & snacks lunchtime & evening*
Restaurant, Garden

THE KING'S HEAD
115 UPPER ST, N1

The big gaunt King's Head has been standing since 1864. When Dan Crawford arrived in 1970 – with designs on its billiards room – it, like the whole of Islington, had seen better days.

It's hard to believe now that until the 1970s Islington was run-down and seedy, but it was; and of course, it was cheap too, which was what attracted people like Crawford whose dreams usually exceeded their finances. The King's Head had obviously not seen a lick of paint since its obligatory 1890s remodelling; the billiards room had been used as both a makeshift gym and boxing ring.

Crawford has spent his money where it matters, and the bar is still delightfully seedy, with not much more than some good glass and a gas-bracket surviving from the 1890s. The place is appropriately kitted out with old playbills and posters and lit with spots which look as if they were picked up in a theatre closing-down auction. Even the till is pre-decimal, so you have to remember things like £1.12s being £1.60.

The theatre itself is a supper theatre: you sit at tables to eat first and then watch the play, although there are also 40-odd ordinary seats rescued from the Scala (Marylebone, not Milan). Watch carefully: the unknowns performing before you could be tomorrow's Tom Conti, Ben Kingsley, John Hurt, Alan Rickman or Kenneth Branagh, all of whom trod these very boards in their salad days.

OPEN *all permitted hours*
STATION *Angel/Highbury & Islington tube*
BEERS *Carlsberg-Tetley range*
FOOD *snacks lunchtime; evening meals for theatre-goers only*

THE NARROW BOAT
119 ST PETER ST, N1

CANALS have been, until recently, perhaps the most underrated feature of Britain's industrial heritage. Expensive to keep open and commercially redundant, canals have for years posed a problem. Holidaymakers wanted to use the most picturesque rural stretches; but that meant that in order to maintain viable networks, the dreary, unloved, urban locks and basins with their crumbling derelict warehouses had to be maintained.

In the last decade, though, developers have looked beneath the grime and decay and discovered the beauty and potential of urban canals and their surviving buildings. In all of Britain's major cities, luxury flats, restaurants, grand hotels and prestige offices and studios have been carved out of the Victorian solid.

Throughout, a handful of canalside pubs have survived, patronised by the bargees and their families in the glory days, discovered by generations of tourists once the commercial traffic had gone, and now beloved of the affluent young urbanites who have moved into the neighbourhoods. Few of these canalside pubs are more charming than the Narrow Boat, overlooking the Grand Union Canal and the narrowboat moorings on Wenlock Basin. Created, from outside appearances, out of a pair of mid-Victorian labourers' cottages, the pub boasts one deceptively large and uncluttered bar, decorated with a moderate amount of period bric-a-brac and maintaining something of a cottage atmosphere.

An extension intended for dining is unashamedly gimmicky: it is actually shaped like a narrowboat, the matchboarded walls sloping inward from dado level just like the deckhousing of a narrowboat. but there are gimmicks and there are gimmicks, and this gimmick feels quirky rather than kitsch. Leading off the bar is a tiny terrace, not much more than a balcony really, which looks down on the canal basin and has

a wrought-iron spiral staircase leading down to the towpath and more tables and chairs for al fresco drinking.

This is not a grandly historical inn: its architecture is frankly unassuming, and it has no great literary or artistic associations to boast of; this is more modest history, social history perhaps, and on a pleasant evening it will engender in Londoner and visitor alike a real empathy for the humbler, more workaday, side of the capital's past.

OPEN *all permitted hours*
STATION *Angel tube*
BEERS *Bass, Fuller's range*
FOOD *meals & snacks lunchtime & evening; meals evening*
Terrace overlooks canal

THE PHOENIX

ALEXANDRA PALACE, N22

People don't go to the Phoenix Bar in Alexandra Palace for any qualities of its own, but for the fantastic view – surely the finest in London. Ally Pally was built in 1873 as a "people's palace" and park for the burgeoning population – the "ruralising Cockneys" – of the North London terraces which were springing up all around from Stoke Newington to Wood Green. Planned as a pleasure garden on a truly heroic scale, it had a race-course and a trotting course, 196 acres of parkland, and even its own branch line of the Great Northern Railway.

The opening attracted thousands. Two days later the whole place burnt down.

It took two years to rebuild, but the new version was even grander than the old, covering seven acres and boasting a 12,000-seat Great Hall, a 3,500-seat concert hall and a 3,000-seat theatre, art galleries, a museum, lecture halls, library and banqueting suites.

As the only facility of its kind in the city – and possibly the world – it was an immensely popular place of resort in a quarter of London comparatively short of large open spaces. But it was its elevation – it is the highest point in London – which attracted the BBC, which broadcast the world's first high-definition TV service from here in November 1936. The service was suspended during the war and was relaunched afterwards, but from 1956 Ally Pally was used only for news broadcasts, and now only the transmitter remains.

Fire struck again in 1980, destroying half the palace including the Great Hall, the old concert hall (then a roller rink), and the theatre dressing rooms. The south-western end of the building, including the magnificent palm Court with its fountains, pyramids and sphinxes, escaped – and that's where you'll find the Phoenix Bar.

The bar is a modern addition, but in its cool, airy design it admirably echoes the quality of the Palm Court (which, has an 8,000 square metre glass roof). A big horseshoe-shaped bar-counter divides the space, which

is attractively clad in light-coloured wood in the modern style.

Outside, an enormous terrace commands a stunning panorama of the modern towers of London from the high-rise blocks of East London, taking in Canary Wharf Tower, the NatWest Tower, the triple towers of the Barbican, the Crystal Palace TV transmitter, to the Telecom Tower.

OPEN *all permitted hours*
STATION *Alexandra Palace BR*
BEERS *big range including Belgian beers. Traditional cider*
FOOD *meals & snacks lunchtime, snacks evening*

THE WASHINGTON

ENGLANDS LANE, BELSIZE PK, NW4

Very much a local pub, with the big-screen TV tuned permanently to sport, an electronic one-armed bandit emitting loud bleeps and whistles, and no meals in the evening, the Washington wears its grandeur lightly.

The present decorative scheme can be dated to the early 1890s by its glasswork, which was carried out by the firm of Walter Gibbs using a process introduced in 1891. That doesn't invalidate the pub's claim to date from 1830, though: what often happened in the pub-building boom of the '90s was that older pubs, which tended to comprise a single big room, were divided into smaller, more private snugs by the introduction of ornate partitions of intricately-embellished glass and mahogany. The best-known example of this is the Argyll Arms in Oxford Circus, a pub of 1868 whose breath-taking mirrored partitions were inserted in 1895.

What has happened since then, in most pubs, is that the partitions have been removed to recreate the single big bar – which, of course, can accommodate more drinkers. Here at the Washington, one of the splendid partitions from the 1890s survives complete, creating a separate public bar; the bar-back also dates from the 90s, as do the entrance lobbies and much of the glasswork.

But it's the windows which give the Washington its rather sombre grandeur. Unlike other pub windows of the period, which are usually composed of a single plate of opaque decorative acid-etched glass, the Washington has giant clear-glass sashes which may well be the 1830 originals. Somehow these windows create the atmosphere more of a great country house library than of a North London local – an atmosphere which must have been appreciated by the street's most famous inhabitant, the fey illustrator Arthur Rackham, who lived in an equally fey little cottage in Chalcot Gardens just opposite.

The Washington boasts in gold lettering above the magnificent black marble pilasters of its facade that it is "a splendid public house". Quite right.

OPEN *10-11 (early for giant breakfasts) mon-sat, 12-10.30 sun*
STATION *Belsize Park tube*
BEERS *Carlsberg-Tetley range*
FOOD *meals & snacks lunchtime, snacks evening*

SOUTH LONDON

The great Thames was for centuries a barrier to development south of the river. Southwark is the only area to the south that really has a London history. It was the southern terminus of London Bridge, for a long time the only point of crossing.

Here inns and taverns blossomed to serve travellers and pilgrims as they approached the city. Southwark's independence from the city authorities also allowed for the development of the theatres of Shakespeare and Marlowe - the Rose, the Swan and the Globe. They of course had their attendant inns, in one of which Marlowe was killed.

What we now know as south London is really a disparate collection of villages drowned by the 19th century urban sprawl. Thankfully it still has acres of glorious open space: Richmond Park, Wimbledon Common, Putney Heath, most of them dangerous, bandit-infested wasteland until 200 years ago, but now providing a vital breathing-space. Then there are elegant residential areas too such as Barnes, Dulwich and Greenwich. Many of these open spaces and old villages have a wealth of good pubs steeped in history. A selection of the best follows.

Opposite The Windmill on the Common – once a traveller's respite from highwaymen

ANCHOR TAP
23 HORSLEYDOWN RD, SE1

Horsleydown Road and its gem of a pub are dominated by the shell of the old Anchor Brewery, the last of the great breweries in an area once renowned for them. Southwark was the gateway to London for hops coming up from Kent and the former Hop Exchange still stands in Borough High Street, alongside the ornate offices of long-forgotten hop merchants.

The Anchor Brewery existed from Tudor times until the early 1980s, when its owner Courage finally closed it. The original Anchor Brewery was not sited here at all, but on the western side of what is now Tower Bridge Road. In the late 18th century it belonged to the Thrale family, who were great patrons of Dr Johnson and let him use a room in the brewery while he was compiling his dictionary. It was on the occasion of the sale of the brewery to Barclay Perkins in 1781 that Johnson remarked: "We are not here to sell a parcel of boilers and vats, but the potentiality of growing rich beyond the dreams of avarice."

Three years after Johnson's death, in 1787, an entrepreneur of Huguenot descent, John Courage, was embarking on his own dream of avarice, acquiring the present Anchor Tap – his first pub – and building his own Horsleydown Brewery at the riverside end of the street.

It was not until 1955 that Courage acquired Barclay Perkins, upon which the original Anchor Brewery was closed and pulled down, and its famous name was transferred to Horsleydown.

The old Anchor Tap has arrived at the present day pretty much in its late 18th-century guise, a Wharfland treasure of dark oak, nicotine-coloured plaster, high-backed settles and cosy little snugs in the very shadow of Tower Bridge.

OPEN *all permitted hours*
STATION *London Bridge BR & tube*
BEERS *Sam Smith's range*
FOOD *meals & snacks lunchtime & evening*
River terrace

THE COUNTRY HOUSE
2 GROTON RD, EARLSFIELD, SW18

It would be nice to say that London's inner suburbs were speckled with unspoilt little late-Victorian locals like this; sadly, they aren't. There are dozens, if not hundreds, of corner pubs of Victorian origin, it is true; but few express their roots as clearly as the Country House.

The little enclave of workshops and artisans' cottages at the crossing point of the River Wandle and the railway which make up Groton Street and Thornsett Road was developed at about the turn of the century. Before that, it was one of those fringe areas where industrial development had encroached on and blighted ancient farmland without yet totally submerging it.

In maps of the 1870s, a dye-works perched on the edge of the Wandle (and doubtless turning it some interestingly unnatural colours) co-exists uneasily with a scatter of farm-labourers' cottages and other humble buildings – one of them almost certainly the beerhouse which still exists today.

If the pub really is, as its name suggests, 20 or 30 years older than its surrounding buildings, it would not be unusual: pubs, like churches, are frequently older than their surrounding habitations, the reason being that if they were still profitable working buildings when their old neighbourhoods were developed, the spec builders were happy to let well alone.

The Country House today exhibits every sign of having been the perfect local for a good 120 years: a corner site of pretty and well-kept appearance, it has exactly the plush lounge with panelled dado and rather simpler public bar with high-backed benches that one would expect. Unself-consciously a back-street local, it epitomises a style of pub

which was once universal but which has now been so knocked-about, converted for other use, or even demolished as to be a museum-piece.

The Country House has no particular claim to historical fame, but it does have one of those endearing little eccentricities which often mark out old pubs. Its location almost next to Earlsfield Station explains its nickname (The Fog): commuters used to pop in, call home, and say they were stuck in the Fog.

OPEN *12-11*
STATION *Earlsfield BR*
BEERS *ScottishCourage range*
FOOD *meals & snacks lunchtime & evening*

THE CROOKED BILLET
14 CROOKED BILLET, SW19

The lesser-known of the two Young's pubs on this little street, but unquestionably the older, the Crooked Billet was first recorded as an inn and brewery in 1509, and, like the site on which the Green Man at Putney now stands, was the property of the family of Henry VIII's chief minister and architect of the Reformation, Thomas Cromwell. His father is recorded as having died here in 1513, and the pleasant little green opposite was once known as Cromwell's Half Acre.

Cromwell made his mark as a merchant in the early part of the reign before becoming a Member of Parliament and financial adviser to various noble households including that of Thomas Wolsey, Archbishop of York, whose right hand he soon became.

Learning nothing from the downfall of his master, Cromwell became the King's private secretary in 1534, steering through the Commons the various Reformation Acts, and personally overseeing the supression of Britain's monasteries in the late 30s. His career, like Wolsey's, foundered

on Henry's impossible marriage policy: Anne of Cleves, a Protestant German princess, was an impeccable choice, politically speaking; but for the "Flanders Mare" to succeed Jane Seymour, who had died giving birth to Edward VI and whom Henry still mourned, was too much to expect. Anne went home; Cromwell to the block.

The pub you see today has been entirely rebuilt since then, probably more than once. It is composed of two buildings: a substantial house of the late 18th century with an adjoining cottage which was probably originally a mews, since it is partly built over the coach arch. Inside, there is a big L-shaped bar with bare floorboards and bare brick wall, furnished with four-square Jacobean-style chairs and settles, with a stone-flagged restaurant area to one side. It's all very olde-worlde, but in fact the decorative scheme only goes back to 1994 – which only goes to show that there are as good pub designers around today as ever there were. If only Young's would lend some to other brewers!

The name is one which has been allotted more interpretations than almost any. The thing to remember is that a billet is almost any straight-ish piece of wood, from a club to a piece of firewood; and "crooked" in medieval English can mean crossed just as easily as bent. Pubs called Crooked Billet very often carry a saltire on their signboards, which leads us either to the Neville coat of arms (and the Nevilles were huge landowners), or to the saltire of St Andrew, the patron saint of Scotland; or (and this is my personal preference) to the saltire of St Julien, a patron saint, along with St Christopher, of wayfarers and hence, arguably, of inns.

OPEN *all permitted hours*
STATION *Wimbledon BR & tube*
BEERS *Young's beers*
FOOD *meals & snacks lunchtime & evening*
Restaurant

FOX & GRAPES
CAMP RD, SW19

This underrated Wimbledon Common pub deserves more attention. Not only is it very pleasantly located – near the centre of Wimbledon Common, with plenty of grassy sward close at hand to sit out on, yet not impossibly far from Wimbledon itself – it also has every appearance of being very true to its roots.

The pub claims a date of origin of 1787, and one look at the symmetrical, sash-windowed main building is enough to confirm the claim. Stepping inside, the older part of the pub is entirely clad in matchboarding, walls and ceiling alike, giving a rustic feeling which is reinforced by the low ceilings and bulky joists carried on square oak columns. This has never been more than a humble country beerhouse, despite the insertion of an arched niche near the bar for the display of good china.

Ironically, the grander and taller of the two bars is to be found in the lower and humbler of the two buildings: the former single-storey stable-block extending as a wing from the old house was converted into a saloon or club-room, open to the rafters and grandly panelled, at some point since the turn of the century, when a photograph now used as a place-mat shows it as still being stables.

One wonders if Jerry Abershaw, the notorious highwayman who plagued Putney Heath and Wimbledon Common in the late 18th century, ever stabled his horse here? Abershaw was hanged in May 1798 and gibbeted on the knoll at the north end of the Common still called Jerry's Hill. Pitt the Younger and William Tierney, MP for Southwark, fought a duel in the shadow of his swinging corpse: standing 12 paces apart, both fired twice, and neither of them having the slightest

experience of firearms, missed completely – they were more likely to hit poor Jerry than each other, not that he would have noticed.

The proprietors must have been greatly relieved, and indeed enriched, when the likes of Abershaw were no more: from being a notorious place to avoid, the Common became a place of very popular resort. The old iron-age earthworks were rediscovered and attributed to Caesar; the windmill was treated for woodworm and given a coat of paint; and the Fox & Grapes, as the above-mentioned place-mat reveals, started doing teas.

OPEN *all permitted hours*
STATION *Wimbledon BR & tube*
BEERS *ScottishCourage range*
FOOD *meals & snacks lunchtime & evening*

THE GEORGE
77 BOROUGH HIGH ST, SE1

The single wing that survives of the George is also the sole remaining representative of Southwark's – and indeed London's – once numerous galleried coaching inns. On either side of the George are memorials of vanished contemporaries; on one side is White Hart Yard, site of the White Hart mentioned by Shakespeare in Henry VI, and the place where the Pickwickians first met Sam Weller in Dickens's *Pickwick Papers*; on the other side is Talbot Yard, where once stood the very Tabard itself, point of departure for Chaucer's pilgrims.

Now they are gone, as are the Belle Sauvage, the Golden Lion, and countless others, and all that is left of the whole species is one third of one of them. Understandably, the George now belongs to the National Trust.

The inn is first known from John Stow's *Survey of London*, published in 1598 when Southwark was an unregulated stew notorious for brothels and bear-baiting. It is said, with what authority I do not know, that the young Shakespeare acted from the back of a cart in the yard before the Globe was built.

The present building dates from 1676,

when it was rebuilt after a fire. Standing as it did on the only route into and out of London from the south, it was one of many inns which profited greatly from coaching: at its peak it entertained 80 coaches a week. These inns had a captive market in travellers arriving after sunset, when London Bridge was closed.

It was still a great inn when Dickens knew it – he mentions it in *Little Dorritt* – but soon afterwards the railways came. They did for the George's rivals; they nearly did for the George, too, for the two vanished wings were pulled down in 1889 by the Great Northern Railway Company to make way for engine sheds.

What is left is enough to be going on with. A maze of bars crammed with dark oak, all benches and settles and smoke-stained plaster, the George and its vanished fellows are best described by Dickens himself.

"Great, rambling, queer old places they are, with galleries, and passages, and staircases, wide enough and antiquated enough to furnish materials for a hundred ghost stories."

What Dickens would have made of the truly awful new buildings round the other sides of the yard we can probably guess; heaven knows how they came to be built. If you visit the George on a fine enough day to sit in its old yard, sit with your back to these monstrosities and drink in the vision of the great, rambling, queer old George.

OPEN *all permitted hours*
STATION *London Bridge BR & tube, Borough tube*
BEERS *Whitbread range plus many guests*
FOOD *meals & snacks lunchtime & evening*
Restaurant

THE GREEN MAN
PUTNEY HEATH, SW15

With the coming of the railway in the mid 19th century, South London suddenly exploded. In a period of not much more than 50 years, suburbs with populations of 100,000 and more grew up where previously there had been parishes whose electoral rolls had scarcely made double figures. The most dramatic example, Penge, saw its population grow from around 20 in 1850 to 180,000 in 1881; Surbiton, Woolwich and other southern hamlets saw similar if somewhat smaller increases.

As the brown-brick terraces spread themselves unchecked over the rolling wooded countryside, so places like Putney Heath became ever more precious. Within living memory the area had been a dangerous one where highwaymen (a romantic rendition of the term "mugger", which fits most highwaymen pretty well) operated almost without constraint. A map of 1816 shows Richmond Park, Wimbledon Common and Putney Heath as contiguous open spaces, unfarmed and uninhabited save for the odd row of cottages, and feared by all who had to cross them.

The transformation of the landscape effected by the growth of the new suburbs led to a transformation in people's appreciation of the few remaining open spaces. Once a place to be shunned, Putney Heath became a welcome place of resort, and the Green Man (the name referring either to the verderers who once maintained the place or the nature-spirits who haunted it, depending on your bent) changed from an agricultural labourers' beerhouse to tourists' watering-hole.

Not that much has changed in the last 130 years, really. The Green Man is still a popular place for walkers on the Heath as well as locals, and little has changed since it was built in about 1700. It's a simple two-bar pub whose basic decorative scheme of bare timber and cream-coloured plaster was probably last altered in the 1880s or 90s, with beer gardens at the front and to one side and, that rarest of survivals in London, an outdoor gents. It may not be a rural pub by the standards of those who live deep in the countryside, but to South Londoners in search of a tonic, it certainly hits the spot.

OPEN *all permitted hours*
STATION *Putney BR, East Putney tube*
BEERS *Young's range*
FOOD *meals & snacks lunchtime & evening*
Garden

Above The Green Man still has beer delivered by horse and dray

HAND IN HAND
6 CROOKED BILLET, SW19

The Hand in Hand is very much the junior of the two Young's pubs overlooking this pleasant fragment of the green. Made up of two pairs of early 19th-century cottages (one of them originally a bakery) round two sides of a small patio, it has been a pub since the 1870s – or at any rate, it has been licensed since then: it's more than likely that part of it was a beerhouse during the period 1830-1869, when no licence was necessary.

The pub was in private hands until Young's bought it in 1974 (which must have been irritating for Watney's as the site once belonged to its founder's grandfather), knocking all the little rooms and snugs pretty much into one.

With its quarry-tiled floors and carved wooden benches, it has a less formal feel than the Crooked Billet, and despite being effectively one big room it still has an atmosphere of cosiness and intimacy.

The one part that is detached is the no-smoking snug converted out of what seems to have been an old shed, or perhaps a barrel-store, on the third side of the patio. Children are welcome in this room, where there are various games to keep them amused.

The most important drinking areas at the Hand in Hand are not inside but outside. The patio faces south and gets plenty of sun, but is pleasantly shaded by a middle-aged horse chestnut, it also has a veritable florist's-worth of window-boxes and hanging baskets.

OPEN *all permitted hours*
STATION *Wimbledon BR & tube*
BEERS *Young's range*
FOOD *Meals & snacks lunchtime & evening*
Family room
Garden

THE ORANGE TREE

45 KEW RD, RICHMOND, TW9

Undoubtedly the best-known pub theatre in London, the Orange Tree was also the first, the upstairs room hosting its first performance in 1971. Actually, that's not quite true: as early as the 16th century itinerant companies put on performances in inn-yards (Shakespeare himself acted on a hay-cart in the yard of the George, Southwark), a tradition which continued in country districts into the 19th century.

In early Victorian times, many London pubs had concert-rooms or theatres attached, perhaps the best-known of them being the Eagle in City road, whose theatre was known as the Grecian, and the Old Vic in Lambeth, originally the Royal Victoria Tavern. The Museum Tavern in Bloomsbury was designed by the architect William Finch Hill, whose stock-in-trade was pubs with music-halls attached. The separation of legitimate theatre from pub-theatres and music-halls came about through the Theatres Act 1843, which banned smoking and drinking in the auditoria of "straight" theatres.

All this had died out by the 1890s, but the Orange Tree always had a theatrical clientele: the Green Room Theatre Club was based here in the 1920s, and the paintings of the Seven Ages of Man by Henry Stacey Marks were presented to it in 1921.

The pub's theatre soon became a proving ground for experimental or new plays, many of which transferred to the West End; and high-profile actors were happy to work here. So popular did the theatre grow that in 1989 it moved into the old school in the adjoining side-street; but the pub's own upstairs room is still in use as well.

The pub itself is a handsome Flemish-baroque building of 1897, which replaced a pub at least a century older (and possibly more, since the orange element in pub names is often associated with William III, who ruled 1688-1702). It is built of pink brick banded with white stone, having a ground-floor frontage of highly-polished black Aberdeen

granite and cupolas and an ornate gable decorating the roof-line.

Inside, the bar is cavernous, although the number of fireplaces betray how many rooms it contained before it was opened up. The rather ponderous mahogany bar-wagon and the weighty gantry are almost the only survivals of the original fittings.

OPEN *all permitted hours*
STATION *Richmond BR*
BEERS *Young's range*
FOOD *meals & snacks all day except sunday evening*

THE PHOENIX & FIRKIN
WINDSOR WALK, DENMARK HILL, SE5

The Phoenix & Firkin is a monument to a truly remarkable entrepreneur. The pub was born out of the ashes of the 1866 Tuscan Palladio-style ticket office of Denmark Hill Station, burnt down by an arsonist in 1980. At first British Rail wanted to demolish the remains, but a public outcry led to second thoughts, and in the end BR polled commuters on what to do with it.

They voted for a pub, so BR put the job out to tender – and every one of the established brewers shook their heads. Enter David Bruce, the former Theakston's of Masham brewer who a couple of years earlier, in revulsion at the poor standard of pubs and beer then prevalent in the capital, had founded his own chain of home-brew pubs, the Firkins.

Two years later the Phoenix arose, complete with a model railway running round the bar, a viewing gallery, a brewery in the cellar, and a huge double-faced clock liberated from Llandudno Junction Station. It was a tremendous breath of fresh air and was an overnight sensation. In 1989 David Bruce sold his little empire, eventually to Allied – one of the very brewers David had set out to subvert. There are now some 150 Firkins, and the number is set to double; but the daft names and dreadful puns are all they have in common with Bruce's Firkins.

They are no longer music-free environments in which conversation can flourish, and their beer is exorbitantly priced. Whereas Bruce started out from a sense of history, a knowledge of what pubs should and could be, they plaster the Firkin theme over pubs at random and without respect, wrecking some of Britain's most venerable inns and taverns in the process.

They have not wrecked the Phoenix & Firkin, though. It is still clearly the work of an inspired individual, rather than a piece of theming off the corporate peg. The sense of fun that hangs about the madcap choice of memorabilia is a real sense of fun, not a contrived pastiche supplied with theme accessories from a central warehouse.

OPEN *all permitted hours*
STATION *Denmark Hill BR*
BEERS *Firkin range plus guests*
FOOD *meals & snacks lunchtime & evening.*

THE SPREAD EAGLE
71 WANDSWORTH HIGH ST, SW18

Wandsworth has been an important centre of brewing since the 17th century and, as the home of Young's, boasts so many splendid pubs – the Alma, the Old Sergeant, the Young's Brewery Tap itself – that choosing the right one for inclusion is very hard. After many contemplative pints, the Spread Eagle emerged as the winner for its pure unashamed magnificence.

There's something about it which is more expressive of the Young's character than some of the company's better-known pubs in the area. Like flamboyant chairman John Young, the pub is extravagantly upfront, with its stained-glass port-cochere straddling the pavement. Inside, its big public bar and truly cavernous lounge are divided by original and ornate glass and mahogany partitions. As with the company itself, remnants of the Victorian original – the Cameoid pressed-paper ceiling, for instance – give colour and character to a very modern business operation.

And like Young's, the Spread Eagle stands on ancient foundations. Completely rebuilt in 1898, it replaced a coaching inn which had stood on the site since at least 1780 and probably much longer, and which Young's acquired as long ago as 1836.

The old Spread Eagle was a considerable establishment, and at the very heart of its community. As well as its extensive stabling, it boasted a tea-garden, a ballroom, a separately-licensed tap, and an assembly-room which doubled as a concert hall until 1900 and later became the area's first cinema.

From 1874 bits of the site – surplus to requirements now coaching was well and truly dead – were progressively sold off. Part became a bank; part was sold to the Public Works Department; part became the Wandsworth County Court – a natural development, since before 1860 the magistrates had sat in the pub anyway.

Although the Spread Eagle was altered and greatly opened out in the 1980s, it still retains the grandeur of the former 1898 rebuilding.

OPEN *all permitted hours*
STATION *Wandsworth Town BR*
BEERS *Young's range*
FOOD *meals & snacks lunchtime & evening*

THE WINDMILL ON THE COMMON
CLAPHAM COMMON SOUTHSIDE, SW4

The windmill is long gone from Clapham Common and so, thankfully, is the rather bogus "Ye Olde" prefix which used to disfigure the pub of the same name. The truth is that this splendid hotel – it's one of the few London pubs to boast letting rooms – isn't all that "Ye Olde" at all. It was once, to be sure: the windmill is recorded on the site as early as 1655, and at some point the miller, one Thomas Crenshaw, went into the alehouse business too.

As well he might, for the road from Lambeth to Merton Abbey was a long, dry one, and dangerous too (the Common, like most open spaces surrounding the capital, was prime territory for highwaymen), and a halfway halt for a beer must have made the remaining half of the journey much easier to face.

By the mid 18th century the grinding corn side of the business had been quietly allowed to drop as the victualling became more successful. The inn, described by one customer as "a very genteel and good-accustomed place", became a posting-house as well as a wayside resting-place; once a year it was a popular house of call for crowds returning to London from a day out racing at the Epsom Derby, even appearing in the background of J F Herring's painting, "Return from the Derby," now in the Tate.

The founder of Young's brewery knew the inn well, his family having lived almost next door; and in 1848 took over the lease of it, 17 years after setting up in business at Wandsworth. Half a century later, the brewery bought the freehold, and rebuilt the Windmill in pretty much its present form.

It is composed of two big and fairly plush bars, the back room having an interesting roof in the shape of a flattened four-cornered Byzantine dome, with little lights in the transoms. There is also a pleasant airy conservatory, which Young's has made a smoke-free zone. There is also a pleasant, airy and fairly smoke-free garden: Clapham Common.

OPEN *all permitted hours*
STATION *Clapham South tube*
BEERS *Young's range*
FOOD *meals & snacks lunchtime & evening*
Restaurant
Garden
Disabled access

INDEX